A12-50

CW01072770

Christopher Rowe

The Management Matrix
The Psychology of Interaction

ALFRED WALLER LIMITED

Published by
Alfred Waller Ltd, Publishers
Orchards, Fawley, Henley-on-Thames
Oxfordshire RG9 6JF

First published 1992

British Library Cataloguing-in-Publication Data.
A catalogue record for this book is available from the British Library.

ISBN: 1-872474-02-0

Produced for the publishers by
John Taylor Book Ventures
Hatfield, Herts

Typeset by Nene Phototypesetters Ltd, Northampton

Made and printed in Great Britain
by Printhaüs Book Company Ltd, Northampton

Contents

Biographical note

Christopher Rowe has degrees in social science and is a Master of Philosophy in Management Studies. He trained as a teacher and has spent over twenty years teaching at various universities, polytechnics and colleges. In the 1970s he moved into management education – teaching on a range of courses up to MBA level and undertaking consultancy for various companies – and, in 1990, became a full-time trainer for British Aerospace. He has published over a hundred journal articles on various aspects of management and the human aspects of information technology. In 1990, the second edition of his book *People and Chips: The Human Implications of Information Technology* was published by Blackwell Scientific.

Preface

After twenty three years teaching in education – most of this concerned with business and management studies – I switched to industry and became a management trainer with one of Britain's largest manufacturing organizations. This book has come about as a result of that switch. I came to see, far more clearly, the problems that managers face in relating theory to practice and to appreciate the shortcomings of much management training. Consequently, this is not simply a book about management, but more specifically about training.

The move from education was illuminating. Not only did I have to get used to different terminology – presentations, delegates, syndicates and training instead of lectures, students, tutorials and education – and a new work environment and culture, but I also had to adjust my techniques to a different learning situation.

It is with these issues that this book is primarily concerned. My hope, therefore, is that it will be of interest and value to three different audiences: firstly, students and delegates on supervisory management courses; secondly, lecturers and trainers trying to present such courses; and thirdly, those with a general interest in management issues.

I am grateful to my many friends and colleagues, both at British Aerospace, other companies and in the educational world, who have influenced this book and to the students and course delegates who have honed so many of my ideas and given me the chance to expound them. In particular I am indebted to Dr Susan Dellinger whose seminar on management effectiveness first sparked my interest in 'the shapes'. Finally, I am grateful to Alfred Waller, Neville Gosling, John Martin and Keith Allen who were kind enough to read early drafts. Their comments have been invaluable, and I have incorporated many of them but, in the last analysis, all the views expressed remain my own.

Christopher Rowe

1 Introducing the matrix

'I'd like you to pick a shape. Any shape. The shape that you feel is "you"'.

Figure 1.1

This is something I was asked to do recently at a management seminar. We were told it was 'psycho-geometrics' and that the shape we chose said something about our personality. But I had my doubts. It seemed to me more like 'psycho-astrology': the idea that a shape reflected my personality seemed as questionable as the suggestion that Leos are jolly or Virgos unreliable!

And yet it highlighted a central question that pervades management teaching (and the whole of Psychology for that matter) and was to provide me with a useful vehicle for considering management issues. 'To what extent *are* we similar and to what extent are we different?' Physically, for instance, we are similar in many respects – we have one head, one heart, two legs, two arms, etc. – but it is also clear that, between people, there are enormous variations in height, weight, skin colour, shape, etc. The same debate pervades Psychology. On the one hand research shows us that children walk and talk in predictable stages – what we can term the laws of maturation – but it is equally clear that some develop skills (e.g. mathematics, music, engineering, etc.) to a higher level than others. In trying to understand better how people behave, should we focus on their *similarities* or their *differences*? This divide can be seen among those who have written about management. Some (adopting a universalistic approach) maintain that we are *all* motivated in similar ways; that there are *set* stages to decision making; that *everyone* learns in certain ways, etc. While others (who emphasize people's individuality) insist that if people differ in intelligence and physical attributes, why shouldn't they also differ with regard to leadership, motivation or whatever? On traditional management courses the first approach has been dominant, leading to the suggestion that there are psychological *laws* and the notion that one can *teach* topics as skills; i.e. that people can move from a situation where they couldn't do certain things, because they didn't know how, to one where they can. I should declare, at the outset, that this is an approach I find questionable.

The consequence of this approach is that much management education and training, particularly as it relates to people, becomes oversimplified. There are scores of texts which refer to 'the stages of decision making' or 'the characteristics of leadership' as though these were set in stone. I have found myself on many occasions confessing to students that I consider such material simplistic, unrealistic and simply wrong. No doubt this has resulted in many of them wondering whether to believe me or the book but I consider that it is the only honest approach. To my relief, most students too seem unconvinced by this material and point out that 'it isn't like that in the real world'. Unfortunately, however, it can often result in an unsatisfying learning experience for the student. To my mind, the *differences* between people are paramount and too many behavioural courses have underplayed them. A central theme of this book is that we cannot provide precise stages, characteristics, laws, etc. but must highlight the variations in human behaviour.

To be fair, most psychologists (if not management consultants) would agree with me, and have put forward alternative models and arguments. But the result, ironically, is that a situation that was over-simplistic becomes over-complex. We get *too many* theories and viewpoints, many of which are conflicting and contradictory. We have witnessed a plethora of management books – some of which are worthy and original but many of which are repetitive and obtuse – and the problem I find, as a trainer, is that, too often, I end up spouting phrases like 'it all depends on which perspective you adopt', which again leaves students both confused and disillusioned! My aim is to bring some order to the basics of management teaching and to offer a simple model for considering key issues in a coherent way. After all, if instead of saying that everyone is the same, we are now merely saying that everyone is different, are we saying very much?

The use of typologies

It is at this point that we fall back on 'types', and why the shapes I mentioned earlier become so relevant. 'Types' are used in the social sciences all the time for, unless one is able to generalize to *some* extent, one ends up saying nothing. It is an approach that allows us to group people into types (which makes analysis meaningful) while, at the same time, highlighting the important differences between them. Let me illustrate this with a well-known example from Psychology. Hans Eysenck and G. Wilson (1976), when writing on personality, distinguished between two broad types, introverts and extraverts, and suggested that each of us, to varying degrees, approximates to one of these. One can conceptualize this as a 'continuum' ranging from complete extravert at one end of the spectrum to complete introvert at the other (where, in reality, no one will be found), with various points in between. They maintained that through various tests one can identify particular traits which, in turn, form the different types. In later work, Eysenck took this further by claiming that people could also be divided on a further dimension of neuroticism/stability. This allows us to create four main types – stable extravert, stable introvert, neurotic extravert and neurotic introvert.

This approach also introduces us to 'the matrix' – the model for this book – for the four types can be presented on two dimensions, as shown in Fig. 1.2.

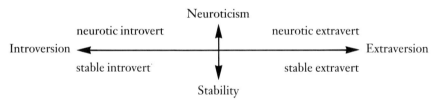

Figure 1.2 Eysenck's type theory

This is often called a '2 × 2 matrix' and is commonplace in social science. Furthermore, it is widely used in quantitative analysis, for it allows statistical tests (e.g. chi square) to be carried out on numerical data – but this is not our concern here. My aim is rather to use the matrix in a similar way to Eysenck and to suggest that the main themes of management teaching, certainly in the behavioural field, can be more effectively understood by means of a matrix – what I shall term 'the management matrix'. My aim is to move away from a highly prescriptive view of management issues; to provide a model which relates the contributions of various writers on these issues into a coherent whole; and to try and bring some order to the vast, wide-ranging literature that now exists. Hopefully, this will provide a more straightforward approach to management teaching. I believe that mine is an approach that can prove equally effective with managers at different levels, in different functions and in different organizations.

Getting into shape

We must now return to the shapes. We were assured that the shape we chose did, to some extent, reflect our personality, and that the shapes were representative of particular characteristics.

(a) The *square* is a hard worker, well organized, dependable, cautious, meticulous, knowledgeable and good on long-term projects. But squares need to be given clear guidelines and appropriate tools. They are not strongly oriented towards people, are content to work on their own on detailed projects and are generally happy with their own company. On a training course a square is the sort of person who takes detailed notes and wants to be sure of gathering all the necessary information. This is not the shape of the leader but rather the reliable lieutenant.

(b) The *triangle* is the leader shape. Triangles love recognition, are conscious of the organizational hierarchy, and are confident, decisive and clear where they are going. However, they can also be outspoken, dogmatic and, at times, stubborn. They are businesslike, conscious of the bottom line, irritated by a lot of detail and prefer summaries to reports. Most important, they often think they can do a job better than others – which means they can be poor delegators.

(c) The *circle* is chosen by those who are people-oriented. Unlike the first two shapes, this has no rough edges: it is a warm shape, resembling the sun, and adding two eyes and a mouth can give you a happy smiling face! Such people are harmonious, likeable, nurturing, emotional and good communicators. Moreover, in addition to liking others they also like to be liked themselves and work well with people they can get on with. Consequently, they are not always good at being the boss, are suspicious of the organizational hierarchy and can easily be swayed.

(d) The *squiggle* is the one shape that has no set pattern to it: whereas the others take recognizable forms this one differs for every individual. People who choose this shape tend to be different, individualistic, open, creative, innovative, excitable and 'idea oriented'. They tend to look outside the work organization and are adept at coming up with original proposals. But they can also be unreliable, disorganized, scatty, unpredictable and invariably have a low attention span.

The truth, of course, is that, as with Eysenck's types, we may feel we correspond to different shapes at different times; but my experience shows that over 90 per cent of students feel the shape they initially choose is a fair reflection of how they see themselves. Some correspond very closely to a particular shape while others may be more of a mixture, but most seem able to identify with a shape to varying degrees.

I was still not convinced, however, whether such shapes tell us anything about our personality, just as I am not sure whether one can learn anything from a person's handwriting, but I now feel that the suggestion should not be totally dismissed. After all, many firms now request people to handwrite job applications so that they can be analyzed by 'experts' (and there are software programs to quantify the results) while some psychologists even claim to draw conclusions from the way people doodle (Fig. 1.3). For example; notice how different people draw a tree.

| Tree with fruit hanging from its crown | Christmas tree | Large fluffy crown | Large fat trunk and rounded |

Figure 1.3

The suggestion is that such doodles, because they are often drawn unconsciously, reflect traits of personality. What we doodle is an indication of our hidden wishes, longings and apprehensions.

(a) *The fruit tree* suggests a person with an eye for detail. This is a mature personality but as there is a need for self-expression there is a tendency to overemphasize trivial matters.

(b) *The Christmas tree* indicates a person who is mature, reliable, trustworthy, organized and well balanced. This person dislikes detail and trivia and heavy pressure on the lines indicates drive, energy and decisiveness.

(c) *The large fluffy crown* suggests a person who is emotionally responsive and receptive, is non-aggressive and doesn't like conflict. This person enjoys the friendship of others: rounded shapes indicate warmth, affection and friendliness.

(d) *The large fat trunk and rounded crown* shows solid self-confidence, a love of the good things of life, imagination, extravagance, a liking for people and a tendency to show off. Wavy lines show a love of movement, dance and a sense of humour.

How much there is to all this I'm not sure; suffice it to say that the four trees clearly resemble the square, triangle, circle and squiggle respectively.

To return to the seminar; I was, by lunchtime, feeling somewhat irritated. The content of the morning sessions, while entertaining, had been no more than elementary Psychology and I didn't feel I had learned anything new. Nor was I sure there was much to be gained from the shapes. But I was irritated for another reason: the morning had made me think. After all, did it really matter whether there was any truth in the shapes or not? Surely the key point was that, whether we like it or not, (or are aware of it or not) we *perceive* other people as certain personality types and, equally important, they categorize us in the same way. We may not think we are a circle but if others perceive us in that way then that's what counts.

The Johari window

One of the best known models of social interaction, and very useful for our purposes, is the Johari window (Fig. 1.4). The model suggests that each of us,

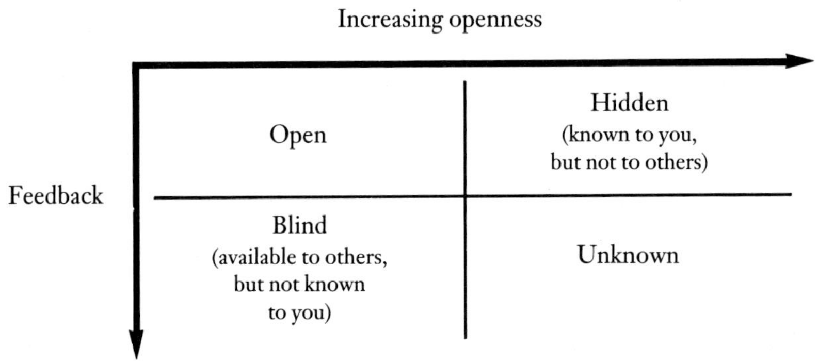

Increasing openness

Figure 1.4 The Johari window

in effect, possesses such a window each time we meet and interact with another person. The top left-hand cell contains the 'open self' – that part of our personality that is immediately visible to another person and which we are unable to conceal. This includes our race, sex, approximate age and what we might term 'presence' (i.e. our manner, dress, posture, etc.) This information is known both to you and the other individual and provides important foundation stones for the interaction.

Up to this point no verbal communication need take place but if one smiles at the other person and passes a few pleasantries then one is 'opening up' one's window. Information that was previously 'hidden' (i.e. known to you, but not to the other person) becomes 'open' as you offer your name, tell the other person about your job, share your interests, etc. In this way the hidden cell becomes smaller and the open cell larger.

But as you offer information to others so it is likely that they too will pass information back to you, about yourself, of which you are unaware. For instance, you may consider yourself shy but other people may tell you that they think of you as highly extravert. This 'blind' information (which is known to others but not to you) provides feedback which allows the open cell to widen even more. During this process the final 'unknown' cell – which provides information that is unknown to both parties and rests in the subconscious – becomes smaller and smaller.

In most situations, if successful interaction takes place, self-disclosure should occur at a similar pace for each individual. We are likely to feel uncomfortable with people who, if we disclose our name, residence, occupation, etc. offer no information about themselves. We consider them 'cold' and comment that 'we can't get through to them' or 'we don't seem to be on their wavelength'. Conversely, we may ourselves 'close up' if we feel the other people are providing their whole life history and candid opinions on every subject under the sun when we have barely met them! In Fig. 1.5, (a) represents a balanced situation, where the participants are each opening their window at the same speed, while (b) illustrates an unbalanced situation with the first person opening up considerably but the other not responding.

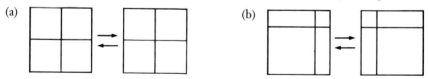

Figure 1.5 Balanced and unbalanced relationships

In some situations, however, an *unbalanced* relationship may work satisfactorily. Obtaining professional advice is a typical example. When we visit our doctor we may well need to disclose personal and sensitive information about ourselves but we would not expect the doctor to do the same. The same point could well apply when dealing with managerial colleagues, particularly if they are significantly senior or junior.

Interaction between the shapes

With the Johari model in mind, and still intrigued by the shapes, I began to ponder the question of how one shape might interact with another. Interaction is clearly a *dynamic* process and just as we respond to various people in different ways so, concurrently, they are responding to us. 'Chemistry' develops – sometimes gloriously, other times, not so – and we find ourselves, in turn, fascinated, bored, maddened, entertained, excited and frightened by other people. Was there, I wondered, a mechanism for considering how the different shapes might interact with each other? This brought me back to the matrix.

Psychologists have long suggested that people can be categorized on two major dimensions – assertion and emotion. Assertive people are 'take charge people' – persuaders, quick decision-makers, extraverts – but they typically have short attention spans. Non-assertive people take decisions slowly, need time to think things over and have long-attention spans. On the other hand, emotional people are likely to take decisions based on *feelings* while those with low emotional levels typically base their decisions on fact. (A way to assess oneself on this dimension is to consider whether you would begin making a point by saying 'I feel' or 'I think'.)

These two dimensions enable us to form a matrix (Fig. 1.6) and to identify four main 'types'.

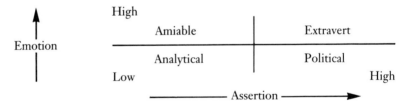

Figure 1.6

(a) The *Analytical* person is neither particularly assertive nor emotional, scoring low on both dimensions, and is the sort of person who can concentrate for long periods, digest large amounts of detailed information and reach firm, calculated decisions.

(b) The *Political* person, being unemotional, is likely to take decisions in a rational manner but, being assertive, is also career conscious, calculating and manipulative, and aware of the political undertones within the organizational hierarchy.

(c) The *Amiable* person, though not assertive, is emotional and people-oriented. Amiable people like to get on with others: it matters that they are liked, and they work well with people they like.

(d) The *Extravert* scores high on both counts, enjoys life and is fun to be with, but can also be unpredictable, disorganized, unreliable, inconsistent and irritating.

It will be apparent that these types closely correspond to the four shapes we discussed earlier. Placing the shapes on our matrix (Fig. 1.7) allows us to consider how one shape might get on with another.

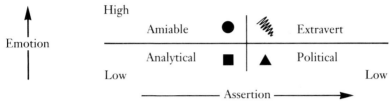

Figure 1.7

(a) *The same shape* Generally speaking, people get on well with their own shape. Political triangles get on well with each other because they both tend to be businesslike, time-conscious, competitive, irritated by detail, etc. Similarly, analytical squares like working with each other because they are precise, detailed, painstaking and accurate; and amiable circles get on well because they are both people-oriented and make an effort to be pleasant with others. Two extravert squiggles simply have a whale of a time.

(b) *The adjacent shape* In many respects people also get on well with those in an adjacent cell. Squares and circles get on well because neither are assertive and don't see each other as 'bossy'; squares and triangles get on because they are unemotional, rational, reliable and accurate; triangles and squiggles get on because they are both outgoing and extravert; while circles and squiggles both like people.

(c) *The opposite shape*   It is with regard to the opposite shape that some of the most interesting observations can be made. Squares are soon maddened by squiggles whom they view as irresponsible, unreliable, and erratic – even noisy and vulgar – while squiggles see squares as 'boring'. Similarly, career-minded, politically astute, businesslike triangles are easily irritated by the soft, smiling, over-emotional, sensitive, woolly-minded circles. In saying this, however, it is important to make a distinction between short and long term. While it is true that people are often irritated initially by those of the opposite shape, many, when they get to know and trust the other person, can become fascinated by them. They come to recognize that the other person possesses many qualities they lack – what we might term 'the attraction of opposites'. Marriage is an obvious example of this. Many couples would confess that they are opposites in many ways and that this provides a real strength in their relationship. This is why, in the long term, a square and squiggle may get on well – with one doing all the entertaining while the other provides a willing audience – while two squiggles may well tire of each other.

In this chapter I have provided a brief discussion of human interaction and suggested that this can be considered in the form of a matrix. This is the main model used throughout the book. I hope it may prove a useful teaching vehicle for those involved in the minefield of management training and, simultaneously, offer a fruitful approach for students wishing to explore key management issues and become acquainted with some of the main writers on the subject. Chapter 2 (What is management?) relates the matrix to the 'management cycle' while Chapter 3 contains a discussion of how managers learn. This provides a framework for discussing the main areas of management training – decision making, groups, negotiation, leadership, motivation, time management, communication and coordination – culminating with a discussion of organizational change and the 'shape of things to come' (Chapter 11).

2 What is management?

The work of Henry Mintzberg

Most management courses begin by posing the question 'What is management?' In attempting to answer this Henry Mintzberg (1973) suggests there have been eight main schools of 'management thought':

1 *The classical school* maintains that managers pursue certain tasks. This follows the work of Henri Fayol and is based on POSDCORB, i.e. the idea that managers plan, organize, staff, direct, coordinate, report and budget.

2 *The great man school* is the opposite, and proposes that the work of managers is best understood by looking at what leading exponents said they did. This avoids the development of general principles.

3 *The entrepreneurship school* derives from economics and views the manager as a rational decision-maker.

4 *The decision theory school* stresses the limitations on rational decision making and focuses on the differences between programmed and non-programmed decisions.

5 *The leader effectiveness school* focuses on the leadership styles that managers adopt.

6 *The leader power school* deals with the politics of interpersonal behaviour and concentrates on sources of power.

7 *The leader behaviour school* studies how managers behave as leaders.

8 *The work activity school* systematically analyzes managers' activities.

This illustrates the wide range of approaches to the study of management. Most can be classed under one or other of these headings but Mintzberg maintains that no single school is adequate in itself (even though they might provide a useful starting point collectively) and this is because they mainly focus on what managers *ought* to do rather than on what they *actually* do. Mintzberg maintains we should concentrate on

★ job characteristics – the way they are characterized by pace, interruptions, brevity, variety, fragmentation, etc.

★ job content – the make-up of management tasks.

★ job variations – the fragmentary nature of many management tasks.

★ job programming – the way in which a manager's job is partly programmed and partly unprogrammed.

Mintzberg then focuses on the important concept of role and three main types of role that he considers managers perform.

★ interpersonal roles – the relationships a manager has with others.

★ informational roles – the ways in which a manager gathers, processes and distributes information.

★ decisional roles – the ways in which managers make decisions that (a) affect the organization, (b) arise from unexpected events, (c) affect the allocation of financial and human resources, and (d) involve negotiation with others.

For Mintzberg this approach provides a more adequate description of what managers actually do than any one school of management thought. The classical writers, for instance are, in his view, far too rigid and precise. Mintzberg's contention is that managers do not simply perform a list of prescribed things – all of which, presumably, have to be performed if one wishes to be a manager – but rather they act out a series of roles. The key to understanding these roles is information: through interpersonal roles managers ensure that they receive information; and by use of decisional roles they utilize it. The central point is that the roles can be put together in various ways by different managers. Mintzberg is concerned with *describing*, not *prescribing*; with focusing on the variety of management activities that can occur. What managers do depends on (a) who they are, (b) where they are, (c) the kind of job they do, and (d) the general environment. Under these constraints, therefore, a particular manager may play one role more than others, play one better than others, etc. There may be certain key ingredients in management that keep reappearing but the 'mix' is constantly changing and it is this that we need to focus upon. This is why Mintzberg's approach is so fertile and is the one I prefer to follow.

Approaches to management

We seem, once again, to have reached the point of saying that 'everyone is different'. But in order to advance beyond this general statement, it is necessary, as in Chapter 1, to classify the various points under four main headings which serve as four approaches to management. To repeat: these do not provide lists of things that managers *ought* to do, but offer *viewpoints* as to what managers think their work is all about. I shall consider each of these in turn.

The science of management
The idea that management is in essence a *science*, involving the study of a precise body of knowledge which can then be acted upon, has been prominent ever since people starting writing about the subject and Frederick Taylor advocated making it 'scientific'. This approach maintains that successful managers are those who have learned an appropriate body of knowledge and have developed an ability to apply acquired skills and techniques. It holds particular appeal for many involved in the provision of management education and training or the supply of equipment to managers for it suggests that there are certain theories, principles, concepts and applications that relate to management and can be taught to budding practitioners. (This corresponds to the prescriptive approach we identified in the last chapter.) The weakness of this approach is that it is patently obvious that one cannot 'manage' a precise set of techniques that can be applied in all circumstances. The reason for this is quite simple: managers have to deal with people, and people are irrational, inconsistent and unpredictable in their behaviour.

The art of management
This, in turn, leads others to suggest that management is more a matter of intuition, imagination, intelligence, leadership skills, native wit and personality. In short, management is an *art*, not a science. Attributes can be developed, but not acquired. This notion – that management is primarily about handling people – has a long tradition in management studies, from the celebrated Hawthorne studies and Elton Mayo, through Likert, Herzberg, McGregor, Argyris, Drucker and many more, to present-day writers such as Peters. Participative, Team, Democratic management – call it what you will – is strongly advocated by such writers and is particularly attractive to

those working in people-oriented areas, such as Human Resources. Many managers, however, are puzzled by the emphasis laid on Human Relations as it seems to them a management style noticeably absent, in practice, from the world of commerce and industry.

The politics of management

The notion that management is the art of getting along with people is, in the eyes of many, too 'soft', for it understates the harsh realities of the business world. Any desire for consultation and participation must be counterbalanced by a need for vision and leadership. Academics may sit in their ivory towers pontificating about 'people skills', so the argument goes, but these are of little use in a fiercely competitive world where the first concern of companies is staying in business. Management may indeed be about handling people; but it is also about competing with them, clashing with them, ordering them, even manipulating or deceiving them, as much as collaborating with them. Conflict, as much as consensus, is seen as characterizing workplaces; and from this viewpoint management is first and foremost about *politics* – the exercise of power in competing for scarce resources. This will probably involve upsetting people and taking nasty decisions; but it is what management is all about. This view is prevalent among managers from small manufacturing companies or those who have to deal with people in political situations (e.g. Sales and Production): they see it as a more realistic view of the business world. Such managers accept and understand the rules and lines of communication in the organizational jungle but are equally eager to discover ways of bending and by-passing them. Intrigue and cunning are part of their make-up; they are politically shrewd, have little interest in academic debates and excel at putting ideas into practice.

The knack of management

A final view accepts that science, art and politics may all play a part in management, but suggests that none is significant enough in its own right to be worthy of detailed study. If management can be viewed in these different ways then it is clearly impossible to define and there is little to be gained in trying. Management is an amorphous label that defies description; and at the end of the day, so the argument goes, is best seen as a *knack*. Certainly there are ground rules that may be learned – one needs to get on with people and it helps to be astute – but how these are combined, or applied in particular circumstances, is a matter of personal *touch*; and while some have it, others haven't. This is the least academic view of management for it suggests that, because the subject-matter cannot be defined, any form of management tuition is of questionable worth. It holds to the belief that managers are 'born not made' and that street wisdom and know-how are developed on the job rather than in the seminar room. This view is commonly held by small businessmen, often with little formal education, who are more interested in doing than studying; prefer to learn by trial and error rather than by reading books; are orientated towards problems rather than ideas; and are interested in results and making things work. Moreover, such managers are likely to be extravert, opinionated, forceful and confident that they are good managers.

Mintzberg would maintain that more managers conform to this fourth view than we might think. He concludes that most managers' jobs are remarkably similar and that their activities are predominantly characterized by brevity, variety and fragmentation. They gravitate towards the current, the well-defined, the non-routine; prefer gossip, hearsay and speculation to routine reports; and tend to deal with specific rather than general issues. He concludes that there is no science in managerial work; it is more a 'seat of the pants' activity.

I would not wish to lay exclusive claim to this fourfold grouping; Watson (1987), for instance, offers a similar breakdown, though he talks of management as 'magic' rather than a knack. But the reason I wish to adopt the four approaches is that they can be applied to the model we discussed in the previous chapter and leads us to the 'management matrix'.

THE MANAGEMENT MATRIX
The first dimension on which we can consider our four 'types' of manager is one that divides between *task* and *people*. Such a division is as old as the study of management itself and goes back to the work of Taylor and Mayo. Taylor and his followers emphasized work study – focusing on the task and making sure that jobs are done in the best possible way with the best possible tools – while Mayo and his colleagues established the human relations tradition in which the worker is seen as a social animal and the effective manager as one who attends to the needs of people. These two approaches provide the central pillars for all later management studies and can, for instance, be clearly seen in the highly influential 'management grid' of Blake and Mouton (1962) where they distinguish between managers who have 'concern for production' and those who have 'concern for people'. This task/people divide is not dissimilar to the emotional/unemotional dimension I discussed in the previous chapter – where we suggested that some could be seen as being more 'people-oriented' than others. If we retain the assertion dimension –

dividing between those we might term passive and those we might consider aggressive – we obtain the matrix shown in Fig. 2.1.

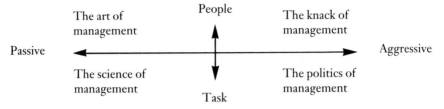

Figure 2.1 The four approaches to management

I am suggesting that the four approaches to management correspond to the four shapes we discussed in the previous chapter. 'Amiable circles' are likely to believe that management is about the art of handling people; 'analytical squares' can be expected to maintain that management is a science that can be studied and learned; 'political triangles' are sensitive to the political aspects of management; while 'extravert squiggles' are more likely to consider management a 'knack'. (Moreover, certain approaches are likely to be more prevalent in certain companies, as we shall see in the final chapter.) But if the management matrix provides the main conceptual model for my book it is the 'management cycle' that provides the *sequence* (i.e. the running order for considering the various topics).

The management cycle

At this point I wish to revert to the classical writers and their suggestion that management involves certain key tasks – planning, organizing, initiating and controlling – and that each of these shares the central core activities of communicating and coordinating. While I reject, like Mintzberg, the suggestion that any single manager *should* do all these we can accept that different managers might do each of these at various times; that some will spend more time on certain tasks than others; and that some will be more effective with particular tasks.

The four key activities can be seen as providing a 'cycle of management elements' (Fig. 2.2) in which management teams keep circulating from one sector to another. This is a popular model on many training programmes and is known as the 'management cycle'.

In most instances the cycle will start with planning and move in a clockwise direction: we can only move to control by going through the stages of organization (providing the resources to do the job) and initiating (motivating, enabling and encouraging people to get the job done). Planning means deciding in advance what needs to be done to achieve a particular objective. This involves, on the basis of forecasts, deciding what to do in broad terms and arranging appropriate strategies. Detailed implementation then takes place in the second stage when human and financial resources are allocated and organized and the policies are put into effect when managers lead, direct and motivate their workforce in the initiating phase. This allows managers to control the situation – to monitor progress, check quality and evaluate developments – which could then lead to further planning.

Figure 2.2 The cycle of management elements

The management cycle, therefore, encompasses the main tasks of management but, in moving through the activities, can we expect different managers to come to the fore? Any manager will, of course, be involved in every aspect from time to time but some can be expected to gravitate towards particular tasks more than others and to indulge in certain forms of behaviour. This is not to say they necessarily perform the task well; merely that this is a stage in the cycle where they like to be involved.

★ The *political triangle*, for instance, is likely to be attracted to the planning stage and the tasks of forecasting, budgeting, developing strategy, etc. This sort of manager is concerned with the big decisions, the broad strategies, and is not too interested in the minutiae. He/she is keen to be involved in key decisions but happy to delegate detailed activities to others. Triangles are commonly found at the higher levels of management and in functional areas such as Sales and Production where managers are often dealing with colleagues in political situations.

⋆ The *amiable circle*, on the other hand, is likely to be interested in organizing people, selecting staff, arranging workteams and counselling others for the changes that lie ahead. Such people are happy to follow the instructions of others and are not greatly attracted to the more entrepreneurial activities of initiating and commanding – indeed, they may well try and avoid them as much as possible. Such managers are valuable to any work organization because they appreciate the 'art' of handling people and may well be found in functional areas such as Human Resources.

⋆ *Extravert squiggles* thrive on new situations, can prove effective motivators and, not surprisingly, are prominent during the initiating phase. (They are prominent in *every* phase but it is here that they can often make a significant contribution.) They will be attracted by new projects and special missions, particularly if they take them outside the workplace and, far from resisting change, positively thrive on it. After all, management to them is a knack; something to be developed as one goes along, not a precise skill to be studied and applied. They are keen to try out new ideas (and are not too depressed if they don't always work) and, like political triangles, keep a high profile, but are far less concerned with power and status. They would rather be thought bright and original than powerful. They are, however, put off by detailed desk work. This sort of manager is commonly found in areas such as Sales and Marketing.

⋆ In the final controlling phase it is the *analytical square* who seems to possess the rational, 'scientific' approach required for monitoring and evaluation. If the work doesn't involve other people to any great extent, and this is often the case, then this is not viewed as a great hardship, for this sort of manager prefers to sift painstakingly through reams of data and prepare and present reports for managerial colleagues. Such managers will adopt a planned, purposeful approach to problems, and can often be found in areas like quality control, research and development, finance and production planning. This is not to say, however, that they always perform these tasks well for, as we shall see in Chapter 9, squares are sometimes *too* meticulous and become hampered by a lack of flexibility.

The message that emerges is that management is a team enterprise (see Chapter 5): that no single manager will, or should, perform every task and that, if they try, they are unlikely to prove good at them. Clearly every manager will be involved in each sector to some extent (e.g. analytical squares may well have an important part to play in the organizing phase) but in certain circumstances we might expect particular managers to come to the fore. Each stage is essential to the overall task and in no way is one better than another. The key to good management, therefore, as with all forms of human interaction, is to recognize and respect our differences.

And yet in many work organizations this is not the case. One constantly hears one department bickering about another – the Accountants about the Salesforce, the Production Department about Human Resources, etc. – or a particular manager moaning about one of his departmental colleagues. These complaints invariably relate to the shortcomings of others and it is significant that managers spend far less time focusing on (a) the strengths of others and (b) their own weaknesses. It is only when we start to do this that we understand management more clearly and improve our own effectiveness.

Does the management matrix, therefore, help us see why managers seem to get on better with some colleagues than others? I think it does. As we noted in the last chapter, people often get on well with their own shape – and departmental colleagues can certainly rally round if they feel they are being attacked by 'outside forces' – but in the long term frustrations can set in, and this may occur where people have worked together for long periods. Similarly, managers can work well with their *adjacent* shapes, for they have much in common. But problems can arise with the *opposing* shape. In my experience, accountants, quality control managers, and research and development staff (analytical squares) are quick to complain about the likes of sales and marketing colleagues (extravert squiggles) who they see as flash, unpredictable, unreliable and erratic, while conversely, sales staff see them as conservative, cautious, nit-picking and boring. Similarly, I have known managing directors who see little case for human resources as a separate function and feel that recruitment, training, etc. can best be shared out between the rest of the management team. Human Resources managers are often seen as 'soft' – out of touch with the hard end of business life – and ill-informed about the product or service that the organization is providing.

For their part, the 'amiable circles' are wary of the ambitious, career-minded, aggressive 'political triangles'. In spite of this, however, each group, as we noted in the last chapter, has a curious fascination for its 'opposite number'. This often exists in latent form, but if managers could more readily accept the contribution and value of others then they would greatly strengthen the effectiveness of the overall team.

What I am establishing is an approach that looks at the *differences* between managers – in the way they handle people, take decisions, manage their time, etc. – and I suggest the management matrix provides a useful model for doing this and for linking the various areas together. But, to repeat, if the matrix provides the model it is the cycle that provides the sequence. I begin, in the next chapter, by considering how managers learn (to provide a basis for later, more detailed discussion) and then, in subsequent chapters, follow the cycle – through planning, organizing, motivating and controlling – round to communicating and coordinating. In Chapter 4 I discuss decision making, so vital for management *planning*. Then in Chapters 5 and 6 I consider how people are *organized* into groups and how they negotiate with each other. Chapters 7 and 8 cover leadership and motivation which are so important for *initiating* activity, while time management (Chapter 9) is discussed as an important aspect of *controlling*. These different functions of management are drawn together by *communicating and coordinating* (Chapter 10) and in the concluding chapter I relate all these issues to a discussion of organizational culture and change. But first, a look at how managers learn.

3 Learning

There are two main schools of thought on learning (the Behaviourist and Cognitive approaches) and these reflect the central debate in Psychology – to what extent are we all the same and to what extent are we all different? Clearly, there are many areas in which we learn in similar fashion (e.g. children in a school class) but the debate revolves around the extent to which we are each unique.

The Behaviourist approach argues that, rather like animals, we learn to respond instinctively to particular situations and, consequently, develop an association between stimulus and response. All experience is stored in our memory and this, in turn, affects future behaviour. The implication of this is that we tend to learn certain skills at certain ages (e.g. walking, talking, etc.) and that there are set patterns for human development.

The Cognitive approach, on the other hand, maintains that humans are very different to animals and that we learn through *mental* processes which are unique to each individual. Our senses do not just receive stimuli but the mind processes them (on the basis of previous knowledge) into *information*. This more individualistic approach to learning is far more in tune with the spirit of my book and is the one I shall adopt in this chapter.

The educational system

For most of us our first association with the formal learning process is through school, and this creates, unfortunately, certain attitudes towards learning. We become conditioned into the belief that learning takes place in the classroom, with the teacher and from the textbook. We are instructed – usually in groups of 20 to 30 with others of similar age and ability – and confirm that we understand this instruction in assignments and examinations. The teacher symbolizes expertise; the textbook symbolizes the assumption that learning is primarily concerned with theoretical ideas and abstract concepts; and the classroom symbolizes that learning is a special activity, cut off from the real world and unrelated to one's life. In all this the student is viewed as the *passive* participant in the learning process. The teacher dispenses knowledge while the student observes, reads and memorizes: far too little time is given to the expressive functions of thinking, writing and oral expression. Textbook learning also implies that the more concepts you can remember, the more you have learned. Concepts come before experience and any application of the concepts will come later. Finally, the classroom suggests that learning and doing are separate activities. No wonder many students at graduation feel they have 'finished with learning' and can now start to 'live'. All this is most unfortunate for prospective managers.

We learn from our five senses – sight, hearing, taste, smell and touch – and of these sight is the most important, followed by hearing, but particularly important is the fact that we learn and remember by *doing* things. A well-known text on learning goes 'I hear and I forget; I see and I remember; I do and I understand', and there is much truth in it. We forget most of what we hear in a formal lecture within a few minutes of its ending and even forget most of the visual images in time. We retain information by making use of it – just as we retain the strength of our muscles by making use of them. Sadly, however, much formal education remains theoretical rather than applied. This, again, is frustrating for the practising manager.

People increasingly recognize that learning is an ongoing process; that it continues throughout life; and that it can take various forms but, unfortunately, our conditioning through the formal educational process often makes it hard for us to accept this. High recognition is still given to academic qualifications, for instance, though it is clear they are merely one sign of effective learning. This is very important when discussing the way managers learn. All the evidence suggests that, while an increasing number of managers are formally trained (through university, college, etc.) there is still considerable *variety* in the way different managers like to learn. Some prefer action, others, observation, still others reflection, and so on. It is to these *differences* that I now turn.

The learning matrix

In an influential piece of work, David Kolb (1971) has suggested four stages in a learning cycle. (Similar work has been done in Britain by Peter Honey and Alan Mumford (1982) and I shall also incorporate some of their terminology.) Kolb suggests that an individual is involved in a concrete experience which serves as a basis for observation and reflection. These are then used to build ideas and form theories which can be tested and applied in different situations (Fig. 3.1).

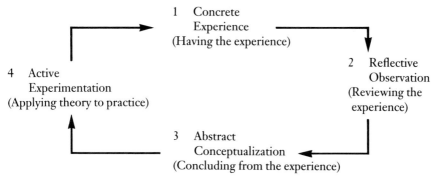

Figure 3.1 Kolb's learning cycle

Each of these stages offers a different learning experience:

1 *Learning by doing* – we gain experience in the real world, concentrating on the real and concrete. Thus, the process *starts* with experience. Some let experiences happen to them (reactive); others consciously seek them out (proactive).

2 *Learning by watching and comparing* – we reflect on that experience and, by observation, compare it to our earlier experiences and those of others.

3 *Learning by theorizing* – we draw conclusions and develop concepts and theories. We indulge in abstract conceptualizations; we draw conclusions from one situation and relate them to another.

4 *Learning by experimenting* – we apply theory to practice. We experiment and test the theory, gain more evidence, and plan the next steps.

Kolb maintains that an individual learning about the world goes through this process time and time again, in spiralling fashion. All four stages are crucial: one has to reflect and theorize in a cognitive fashion, otherwise the behaviour is merely conditioned. Humans learn; they do not simply indulge in conditioned responses.

His key point, however, is that each individual has strong and weak points in the learning cycle. Some are very observant; some are theoretical, others prefer action, etc. Honey and Mumford maintain that no more than 2 per cent score as 'all-round learners': 70 per cent have one or two clear preferences. This produces many stereotypes – the absent-minded professor, the impulsive cowboy, the egocentric actor, the mad scientist, etc. It is because of this, Kolb claims, that people with very different learning styles often have difficulty communicating with each other (e.g. academics and businessmen).

Kolb's argument, therefore, is that we all share these modes of learning – *but to varying degrees.* He suggests that most people are *skewed* towards *two* axes (which provides a matrix with four different 'types') and labels these accommodator, diverger, assimilator, converger. (Honey and Mumford use the terms activist, reflector, theorist and pragmatist.) What he then suggests is that particular learning styles tend to be linked to certain kinds of managerial role (Fig. 3.2).

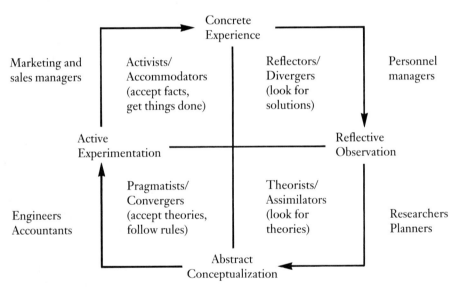

Figure 3.2 Kolb's different learning 'types'

This provides us with four main learning 'types'.

1 *Activists* (active-experimentation/concrete-experience types) These are managers who like problems, actively seek them out and probably favour 'management by walking about'. They adapt quickly to new situations, happily abandon theories and are interested in results and making things work. They like working with people but can be seen as pushy and abrasive. They respond well to direct instruction and leadership, like challenges, have a

tendency to act first and think later, and can quickly become bored with complexity and detail. Marketing and sales managers tend to fit this pattern but so too do many senior and top managers and business studies graduates. Their philosophy tends to be 'I'll try anything once': the aim is to relate practice to practice and learn from experience.

2 *Reflectors* (concrete-experience/reflective-observation types) Reflectors are strong on imagination, can view a problem from many different perspectives and enjoy gathering and reviewing evidence and looking for solutions. They like working with people, are good listeners, but tend to be emotional. They are also careful, thorough and methodical but inclined to be cautious and reluctant to commit themselves early to a fixed view. They are not assertive and learn best by listening to all opinions. They do not easily accept direct instructions. Human Resource managers can be found in this group as can liberal arts and humanities graduates. A favourite phrase of the reflector is 'I'll think about it'. They like to think about an issue and relate practice to theory.

3 *Theorists* (reflective-observation/abstract-conceptualization types) These managers excel at inductive reasoning, at spotting the common factor in a mass of apparently dissimilar cases, and are far more concerned with explanations and theories than people. They are more interested in the attractiveness of a theory than its practical application and are not particularly bothered about results. They are rational, objective, disciplined and methodical, but not very imaginative and can be intolerant of emotion and intuition. They learn best in formal situations and respect intellectual argument, but need to work things out for themselves. This type is common among science graduates and indeed anyone inclined towards an 'academic' approach to learning. In management this person is often found among those who work in areas such as planning or research and development. They are inclined to ask 'How does this fit with that?' and enjoy relating one theory to another.

4 *Pragmatists* (abstract-conceptualization / active-experimentation types) This is the most common type among managers. Pragmatists excel at the practical application of ideas, like to test things out, prefer things to people, accept rules and are unemotional. They are businesslike, oriented towards techniques and procedures, lack interest in theories and underlying principles and are far more interested in relating any theories to practice. They learn

best when given specific instructions by a person whose authority they accept, and enjoy learning new methods and techniques. Engineers and accountants fall into this pattern which is all about relating theory to practice. The pragmatic manager is constantly asking 'How can I apply this in practice?'

To repeat: effective learning involves *all* four stages but Kolb's point is that some people prefer certain styles and are more effective learning in certain ways. He does not suggest that one mode is *better* or worse nor, indeed, that a balanced profile is necessarily best, but rather that the key thing is to be competent in a particular mode *when it is appropriate*. Consequently we need to analyze our strengths and weaknesses – in order to appreciate favourable and unfavourable situations – and this Kolb does in his Learning Style Profile (LSP) test. A high score on one mode may mean a tendency to overemphasize that mode at the expense of others – and vice versa.

Learning and the management matrix

The intuitive reader will already have spotted that our management matrix can be related to Kolb's work, and that of Honey and Mumford. The shapes may be arranged differently from Chapter 2, but each learning style can be linked to one of them (Fig. 3.3).

Figure 3.3 Kolb's learning cycle and the management matrix

I have experienced these types in my own teaching career – particularly when I was lecturing on the Diploma of Management Studies. Activists were common among not only sales and marketing people, but also those who managed small companies. They considered management a 'knack'. The clearest I can recall was a self-made businessman who had once owned a furniture shop and then opened and managed a working men's club on a large housing estate. He was one of the funniest people I have ever met – as well as being one of the most intelligent and articulate – and, on the residential conference, completely dominated proceedings. He was a total squiggle. But, as I feared, he never completed an assignment or exam and, consequently, withdrew from the course. He possessed management skills that most of us can only dream about but the truth is that he learned these by leaning over a bar at three o'clock in the morning talking to a bouncer and a DJ. He would learn from one situation and apply it to another; practice to practice. He operated in a world of street corners, things falling off lorries and fivers stuffed in mattresses. He loved problems, loved people, loved action and quickly became bored with 'academic issues'. The other students will never forget him. He didn't really need academic skills: he already had a first class honours degree from the 'University of Life'.

The course also included, every year, a number of chemistry graduates from a nearby oil refinery. They were invariably superb Reflectors. They rarely said much in class but they listened carefully, respected others' contributions, and were adept at gathering, reviewing and presenting material in an original way. They were not argumentative or assertive and were, consequently, well liked (as is usually the case with circles) by the rest of the group. They were very good at listening to others' experiences and then linking this to a theoretical model (i.e. they related practice to theory). They saw management as an 'art' and usually came top in the exams.

In addition, the course contained librarians from the local library service. Not surprisingly, they were very much at home with books – they were usually able to obtain texts on the reading lists that others couldn't lay their hands on – and were happy extracting material from databases and journals. They were solid squares – or, to use Kolb's label, assimilators – and rather viewed management as a 'science'. Their assignments and exam scripts were always competent and well scripted, but they perhaps lacked flair and did not effectively link theoretical issues to the work situation. Nor did I feel they were terribly interested in anyone else's work situation: one never sensed they learned much about factories.They were happier contrasting one textbook with another; i.e. relating theory to theory. They seemed to enjoy the course; but I was never sure.

Many on the course were Pragmatists (triangles) and they were best represented by managers from manufacturing companies. They were always prominent in the group; were quick to voice their opinions; and were particularly attuned to the political aspects of management. Others found them intimidating at times for they were argumentative, aggressive and quick to lead. They often had an engineering background, were used to a fire-fighting atmosphere and were particularly skilled at relating the theoretical issues on the course to practical aspects of work. They talked a lot about their workplaces and I gained a far clearer picture of their factories than I ever did of the oil refinery or library service. One never felt, however, that they were terribly interested in other work situations but were primarily concerned with talking about themselves. They wanted specific training rather than general education; concrete facts rather than abstract concepts; the experiences of similar managers rather than the 'clever' pontifications of academics; and immediate results rather than long-term promises. They were frequently critical of the course. They also, nearly always, obtained the highest marks for work-based projects.

The implications of Kolb's model

It seems to me that Kolb's model is extremely useful in helping us understand the ways different managers learn and it helps explain why they, so often, seem to be talking past each other. It shows, for instance, why boards are often divisive places: the Human Resources director knows how to use the tools but has difficulty grasping the concepts; the corporate planning manager can grasp the concepts but is not too interested in results; the finance director can apply the rules, but is oblivious to new opportunities; and so on. Each member of the board looks at things from a different perspective.

It also shows why so much management training appears ineffective. The problem is that those who act before they think (if they ever think) are likely to be taught by those who think before they act (if they ever act). Managers thrive on doing and one-to-one encounters while academics are used to formal instruction in group situations. Outside consultants, on the other hand, tend to be Reflectors and, consequently, they too may be mistrusted by many managers.

The message for management trainers, therefore, is that training should be *varied*. Continually changing the learning mechanism is vital. There is a place for the formal lecture (and squares will enjoy it) but it should only be used sparingly and must be accompanied by guided discussion, syndicate work, case studies, T-group exercises, role play activities and business games. The danger with participative exercises, however, is that squiggles will be inclined to enjoy the games *for their own sake* and will insufficiently consider the messages to be drawn from them. This is why they must be accompanied by follow-up and review sessions. In short, programme activities should reflect the whole of Kolb's learning cycle.

For their part, managers should (in response to the above discussion) ask themselves some important questions.

* What learning activities do I most enjoy?

* Are there some styles of learning that I need to improve?

* Are there problems in trying to work with someone who adopts a different style of learning to mine?

* How important is all this if I need to instruct others?

Only by addressing these questions can managers learn effectively and, equally important, help others to learn. The key message is that different people learn in different ways and the important thing is to ascertain strengths and weaknesses – both in ourselves and in others – so that we can build on the former and improve the latter.

4　Decision making

Understanding how managers learn helps us understand how they make decisions. Decision making is vital to the management tasks of planning, forecasting, budgeting, etc. that we identified in the top right-hand quadrant of the management cycle (Fig. 2.2) and yet it is a skill that, by common consent, many managers appear to lack. Some managers simply make poor decisions; others make them too swiftly and without consultation; while others appear incapable of making a decision at all!

Again, I have to confess that I am bemused by much of the textbook material on this topic. It is clearly a complex issue, and one that demands careful analysis, yet so much of what passes for 'decision making training' is simplistic beyond belief. The conventional approach in most course books and training manuals is to present decision making as a *rational* process – the focus is on how decisions *should* be made – and to list the following main stages:

1 *Define* the aim – What is it you are trying to do?

2 *Develop* information – What facts are available?

3 *Refine* the situation – What alternatives are available?

4 *Evaluate* the alternatives – How do the alternatives compare?

5 *Implement* the most appropriate alternative – Which alternative should you adopt?

6 *Follow-up* and evaluation – How effective was your choice?

According to this approach – which is often labelled 'Economic man' – making a decision involves choosing a course of action, in a conscious way, in order to achieve some goal, taking into account such information as is considered relevant and is available. The outcome of such activity is a decision.

We can illustrate the process with a simple example. You might walk into a room that is too dark and decide that you wish to lighten it. You therefore establish the facts and consider alternatives. Are the curtains drawn? Are the lights switched on? Are any candles available? From these you determine the most suitable choice and implement it. If the situation is still not satisfactory (e.g. opening the curtains did not provide sufficient light) then you might modify the situation further (e.g. turn on the lights).

This is a highly systematic, logical approach to decision making – and most management textbooks teach it – but it seems to me wholly removed from reality and virtually worthless. The truth is that, in a work organization – where decisions can involve anything from how many spoonfuls of sugar to put in a cup of tea to making workers redundant – decision making is almost always an ongoing process, where one decision leads into another. There tends to be a *pyramid* of decisions with the most general one at the top (e.g. a major change in policy) followed by less important decisions. In practice, decision making is highly complex, and practising managers, in my experience, can't identify with the rational model because it doesn't relate to the world they experience. They know that different decisions involve different goals, different time perspectives, different strategies of implementation, different information, and so on.

ADMINISTRATIVE MAN

The view that sees decision making as a rational process has been heavily criticized by a number of post-war writers (e.g. March and Simon (1958), Lindblom (1959), etc.) all of whom maintain that we should replace 'Economic man' (the approach that sees the decision maker as a rational, calculating being) with 'Administrative man'. Their approach (which corresponds to the fourth Mintzberg's schools of management thought) maintains that

(a) A manager does not always make the 'optimal' choice, for choices are rarely 'clear-cut'. 'Satisfactory' alternatives are often pursued in preference to 'optimal' ones. For instance, over profit one must distinguish between short-term and long-term, stability, etc.

(b) What is 'satisfactory' often does not depend on technical factors, but on social and political considerations. While Economic man 'maximizes' and is 'comprehensive', Administrative man 'satisfices' and 'simplifies'.

Critics of the rational approach maintain that it is unrealistic to assume that a manager can consider all alternatives objectively: decision makers select and edit from their experience those features they believe to be relevant. In other words, the process is highly *subjective* and optimal solutions are replaced by satisfactory ones. Simon (1947) terms this 'subjective rationality' – managers try to be as rational as they can – and we can also talk of 'bounded rationality' where there are limits to our rational decision-making capabilities. Lindblom sums the whole thing up when he graphically describes management decision making as the process of 'muddling through'. In a later work, John Hunt (1986) has also put it well.

'Most of the time managers do not segment their work into these rational steps. They see, collect information, search their experience (or lack of it) for alternatives, make a decision and go into action. The whole process is over within minutes, even seconds.'

COALITION AND CONFLICT

More recent writers on decision making (e.g. Cyert and March (1963)) have extended the Administrative man approach to see decision making more as a *social* process involving conflict and cohesion. (This corresponds more to Mintzberg's sixth school of management thought.) According to this view, people within organizations are often in conflict but this is counterbalanced by various coalitions (e.g. departments). Similarly, conflict within a depart-ment can lead to sub-coalitions, and so on. Decision making becomes, therefore, not a tidy business but an operation involving constantly changing alliances.

This emphasis on coalition and conflict also moves us away from a view of decision making as an isolated psychological activity to one that, more often, takes place in groups and is political (involving varying degrees of power). We need to focus not simply upon *what* is decided (the actual decision) but also on *how* something is decided (the decision making process). In this respect the work of J. D. Thompson (1967) has been particularly influential.

Thompson's decision strategies

Thompson suggests that decision making can be considered in terms of a matrix, comparing means and ends in terms of certainty and uncertainty (Fig. 4.1).

If outcome preferences and beliefs about cause and effect are certain, then decision making can become a simple *computational* procedure (i.e. a matter of calculation). If preferences are uncertain, but beliefs about cause and effects are certain then a *compromise* strategy may prevail. If preferences are certain, but cause and effects beliefs uncertain then a *judgement* must be made, but if uncertainty exists on both counts, then only *inspiration* can provide an answer. (Such a model is, of course, an abstraction; and it is not suggested that all decisions fit neatly into it, but rather that they will approximate to the different cells.) The first cell corresponds to the 'Economic man' view but the addition of the others shows how decision making is a complicated political process. Management will, presumably, try to maximize the number of decisions where the outcome can (as far as possible) be 'calculated', and reduce dependency on compromise, judgement and, in particular inspiration.

		Preferences regarding possible outcomes (i.e. ends)	
		Certainty	Uncertainty
Beliefs about cause-effect relations	Certain	Computation/ Calculation	Compromise
(i.e. means)	Uncertain	Judgement	Inspiration

Figure 4.1 Decision strategies

Adopting a similar approach, Astley et al. (1982) argue that decision making can vary in terms of complexity and cleavage. Complexity refers to the extent to which the topic is intricate while cleavage refers to the amount of conflict that is generated and involves the political dimension. Where a decision can be 'programmed', levels of complexity and cleavage are low: the decision is likely to be made swiftly and the result is predictable and acceptable to all. Astley et al. illustrate their model with four 'ideal type' examples of decision making (Fig. 4.2).

The lottery decision (case 1) was not a new idea, was not complex, and did not create serious cleavage within the local authority. Conversely, the university committee structure was extremely complex, involved considerable political cleavages, and was only reorganized after considerable debate. If, in such a situation, no agreement is reached, an 'inspired' decision is often imposed by a powerful figure. The models of Thompson and Astley et al. are very similar. Where complexity and cleavage are low, the decision may be more a matter of calculation; where both concepts are high it may well require an inspirational decision; where complexity is low but cleavage high a compromise is likely between opposing factions; and where complexity is high but cleavage low a judgement has to be made.

		Cleavage Low	Cleavage High
Complexity Low	1	Decision by a local authority to introduce a lottery	2 Decision by a subsidiary company to resist head office's new launch
Complexity High	3	Decision by a company to launch a technically complex product in an uncertain market	4 Decision by a university senate to change its committee structure

Figure 4.2 'Ideal type' examples of decision making

Either model corresponds closely to the management matrix, and highlights, I would suggest, the fact that particular managers are effective at dealing with particular types of decision. Where the process is largely a matter of calculation – gathering relevant data, masticating it and regurgitating it as information – squares are in their element. (Many such tasks have now, of course, been taken over by computers.) Where the complexity is high, but cleavage low – as in the case of the new product launch – judgement is required, and here triangles can prove particularly effective. They are well informed, attuned to political considerations and able to take a long-term view. Circles, on the other hand, come more to the fore in situations where complexity is low but cleavage high and conflict occurs between competing groups (i.e. as in the case of the subsidiary company and head office). In such circumstances the circles' negotiating skills and their ability to seek and reach compromises can prove invaluable. Where, however, both complexity and cleavage are high, and no one is sure what they want or how to get it, an element of inspiration is required on someone's part. Enter the squiggle.

DEVELOPING THE MATRIX

I consider Thompson's work a useful starting point for analyzing decision making, but I feel we can go further. If we recall that decision making is an 'ongoing' process (involving sub-decisions) I suggest that the process can be seen, over time, as passing through the different cells. For instance, the decision to install a computer clearly triggers decisions as to what make it should be, where it should be located, who should be trained, etc.; i.e. what starts out as a (supposedly) straightforward decision soon leads to judgement and compromise – even inspiration. The danger of the model as it stands is that it presents a rather static picture and detracts from the *flow* of decisions between the cells as the decision making process unfolds. In my experience, a decision making process often goes from calculation to either judgement or compromise – in which case either triangles or circles come to the fore – and, if nothing is resolved, the squiggles get involved to 'sort things out'.

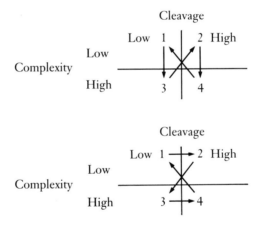

Figure 4.3 Flow patterns through the matrix

Ironically, this supposedly radical intervention is, in reality, invariably an attempt to reimpose a straightforward decision (i.e. to pull the matter back into the computation cell). It often involves someone in a powerful position 'knocking heads together' and 'cutting through red tape' (i.e. outlawing cleavage and reducing complexity) so that a decision can be reached. We can, therefore, detect two routes through the matrix (Fig. 4.3); which one is taken depends on the nature of the problem.

If it appears a *technical* matter (e.g. which make of computer do we buy?)

then the process is likely to move from 1 to 3, as judgements will be needed, and the triangles will be dominant. (We noted in Chapter 2 that triangles can be dominant in all aspects of planning and decision making.) If conflict then develops (and more senior managers become involved) it will move to 2, or even 4 (when top management become involved) before, probably, returning to 1. On the other hand, if it becomes a *political* matter early on (e.g. which department is likely to get the computer?) then the process is more likely to move from 1 to 2 (and then to 3 if various detailed arguments are put forward and specialists called in) before, possibly, moving to 4, and then back to 1. To summarize: I am suggesting that a flow often occurs in decision making; that it can take different forms; and that the particular form it takes is affected by the level of management involved, and the stage at which it becomes involved. Managers of different shapes are also likely to be prominent at each stage.

DECISION TREES

A further approach to decision making – and one that has become influential in management training and is highly relevant for our purposes because it focuses on the flow of the decision-making process – is 'decision tree' analysis, introduced by Vroom and Yetton (1973).

The authors suggest that, depending on circumstances, managers are likely to adopt a particular *style* and offer a choice of five styles ranging from highly autocratic to highly participative:

The five styles are:

1 *Tells* The manager makes the decision alone, using information available at the time (Used on the A1 routes in Fig. 4.4.).

2 *Sells* The manager obtains the necessary information from subordinates, makes the decision alone and justifies the choice (Used on the A11 routes in Fig. 4.4).

3 *Consults* The manager consults relevant subordinates individually and then makes the decision alone (Used on the C1 routes in Fig. 4.4).

4 *Shares* The manager shares the problem with the group but then makes the decision alone (Used on the C11 routes in Fig. 4.4).

5 *Delegates* The manager shares the problem with the group and the group, collectively, reaches a decision (Used on the G11 routes in Fig. 4.4).

Which style a manager adopts in a particular situation is affected, suggest Vroom and Yetton, by four 'decision dimensions'.

1 *The 'Quality' dimension* – Does the *choice* of solution really matter? In some cases any one of a number of solutions may be acceptable, while in others a particular solution may be preferable. (This dimension occurs at point A in Fig. 4.4.)

2 *The 'Information' dimension* – Who is in possession of the *information* necessary to make a high quality decision? Does the manager have sufficient information to solve the problem alone? If not, what information is needed and where can it be obtained? Which individuals or groups should be consulted? (This dimension occurs at point B in Fig. 4.4.)

3 *The 'Commitment' dimension* – To what extent is the *support* of others crucial to a successful outcome? Will a unilateral decision be acceptable or will others' commitment have to be obtained? (This dimension occurs at point D in Fig. 4.4.)

4 *The 'Capability' dimension* – Are others *capable* of producing a high quality decision? Do group members share the organization's aims and objectives? (This dimension occurs at point F in Fig. 4.4.)

This *situational* approach highlights the weakness of rigidly adopting a particular decision style: for Vroom and Yetton claim there is no single style appropriate to all types of decision. The most appropriate style depends on the four decision dimensions and these can be considered in terms of seven questions. (Question A relates to 'Quality': the other dimensions are each covered by two questions.) This provides the decision tree shown in Fig. 4.4: the manager stands at the left-hand side and moves to the right along the path determined by the answer to each question. The model provides 14 possible routes.

A Is one decision likely to be better than another? (If 'no' one can proceed to D.)

B Does the manager have sufficient information to make the decision? (If 'yes', proceed to D. If 'no' proceed to C.)

C Is the problem clear and structured? (If 'no' go for CII or GII.)

D Is it crucial that subordinates accept the decision? (If 'no', then AI or AII are possible.)

E Are subordinates likely to accept the manager's decision? (If 'no', go for CII.)

F Do subordinates share the goals of the organization? (If 'no' avoid CII.)

G Are subordinates likely to conflict with each other? (If 'yes', go for GII.)

It should be noted that all decision processes (i.e. tells, sells, consults etc.) are applicable in particular circumstances and how frequently each is used depends on the type of decision being made. Particular routes are often, therefore, a mixture of different styles.

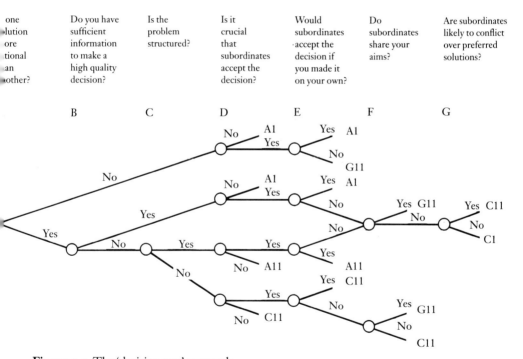

Figure 4.4 The 'decision tree' approach

Figure 4.4 summarizes and simplifies a complex and detailed piece of work – the sophistication of Vroom and Yetton's study can be seen from the numbering of the different routes – but hopefully you can see why their work is labelled 'decision tree analysis' (with the various branches spreading out from the trunk as the process develops) and how some routes are considerably more complex than others. The shortest and slickest route is A1: if all goes smoothly it involves only two stops and is naturally a route that attracts managers wherever possible. But as with the other A1 (the one we drive on) what may appear slick and quick is not always so because other factors (e.g. heavy traffic) affect the situation. We are forced off onto other routes (side roads) and before we know it, find ourselves turning down country lanes we didn't expect! Hence we end up on more complex and detailed routes such as C11 and G11.

In one sense, Vroom and Yetton's model provides a rational approach to decision making – by spelling out the various stages managers must go through – but their main contribution is to highlight the *variety* of paths available and to indicate the circumstances in which one becomes more appropriate than another. The tragedy is, of course, that many managers (influenced by their dominant style) are often poor at identifying the right course and adopting it. Squares constantly want to travel A1 and become frustrated at dealing with extraneous issues. Triangles are good at considering questions B and C but can soon become frustrated with D and E. These (the people issues) are better handled by circles but they are less inclined to consider questions F and G. Squiggles are unpredictable: sometimes they will bludgeon down the A1 while on other occasions they will either crash, get lost, or run out of petrol – failing to reach their destination at all!

5   Groups

Having looked at the manager as a 'planner', we now, in the next two chapters, turn to the manager as 'an organizer' and, in particular, a handler of people. It is the part of the management cycle where we can expect circles to feel particularly at home, though it is an area of vital importance for all managers. After all, management is 'getting things done through people'. Managers spend a considerable amount of time working with others – it has been calculated that, on average middle managers spend 50 per cent of their working day in one kind of group or another, and senior managers, 80 per cent – and the ability to work effectively in groups is essential. Managers need to be able to handle colleagues, superiors, subordinates, customers, suppliers – in short, all kinds of people in various contexts. Anyone who is poor at this is never likely to become an effective manager.

WHY DO MANAGERS JOIN GROUPS?
People join groups because this arrangement provides

1 *Contact with others* – most people prefer some human contact in a work situation.

2 *Social comparison* – it allows us to compare our opinions and abilities with others.

3 *The development of norms* – groups enable us to discover what behaviour is acceptable (e.g. timekeeping, dress, quantity of work, etc.).

4 *Goal achievement* – people like to feel they are achieving goals, both individually and within the group.

5 *Information acquisition* – groups are a major way in which managers find out what is going on.

Typically, managers spend their time in five main types of workgroup:

★ *Command groups* – where managers give instructions to their team. Here there is a dominance of *vertical* communication.

★ *Committee groups* – e.g. health and safety, staff welfare, etc. In such committees there is a preponderance of *horizontal* communication.

★ *Task groups* – groups set up to deal with special problems. Such groups, by definition, have a short existence.

★ *Informal groups* – the various friendship groups that emerge informally within organizations. The other forms of group are all *formally* created (i.e. by the organization) but it has long been recognized that informal groups are equally important.

★ *Reference groups* – the various groups that managers identify with, and compare themselves with (e.g. professional associations), even if they never actually attend meetings.

All these kinds of groups are indispensable to managers in a work situation for they assist the distribution of work, the organization and control of work, problem solving and decision making, information collection and processing, coordination and liaison, negotiation and conflict resolution and motivation and involvement. Groups can greatly enhance individual performance because:

★ the group has access to a greater variety of experiences and skills than does one person. Synergy can occur: i.e. the output from the whole is far greater than the separate contributions of different individuals.

★ by 'brainstorming', groups can generate far more and better ideas than can individuals working on their own.

★ a division of work or effort is possible.

★ groups can generate more information on a problem.

★ members can detect each others' errors.

★ being in on a group decision can arouse the individual's motivation.

★ a sense of trust and belonging can be developed.

Consequently, the performance of simple tasks can be enhanced; groups generally produce *better* solutions; groups are more likely to take *risky* decisions; and people are more likely to carry out a group decision.

WHY DO PEOPLE DISLIKE GROUPS?

Despite this, however, groups are often uncomfortable places. (This is often because managers are never sure precisely which groups they belong to, and sometimes one group can subvert another.) Managers moan of their *ineffectiveness*: the fact that they continually seem to slow things up, create unnecessary conflict, encourage uneasy compromise and frequently produce poor solutions. Managers are quick to point out that 'a camel is a horse put together by a committee' and lament the fact that they spend so much time attending meetings.

Groups can very easily make poor decisions because:

★ The members may be *too* alike/homogeneous; different viewpoints may not be encouraged.

★ The group can fail to detect the skills and experiences of different members.

★ Too large a group (especially with over seven members) can result in restrictions on participation.

★ Attention is only focused on the problem for short time-spans.

★ Peripheral discussions can become time-consuming.

★ The problem may be too technical, complex and known only to a few.

★ Time can be lost because of the social issues (processes) in the group.

★ One member may use coercion, expertise or position to dominate the others and this may eliminate constructive criticism.

★ Conjecture (guesses, rumour, opinion, etc.) can lead the group into irrelevances.

★ Members may be so heterogeneous that they cannot communicate.

★ The group may demonstrate 'group think': i.e. it takes on an identity of its own and members uncritically subscribe to group decisions.

Consequently, on more complex tasks there can be *adverse* effects: tasks can take longer to complete than when individuals are working alone, and brainstorming sessions – in which all ideas are considered – can prove disorganized and ineffective.

As a response to this, management training has spent a lot of time, traditionally, trying to make managers more effective in group situations. Courses have been offered in team building, group dynamics, meeting effectiveness, etc. where the emphasis has been on managers improving their *individual* skills so they might make a more effective contribution. The aim has been to produce the perfect, all-round manager. But any attempt to list the qualities of the ideal manager demonstrates why he or she cannot exist: far too many qualities are mutually exclusive. We expect managers to be intelligent, but not too clever; highly forceful, but also sensitive; dynamic, but patient; fluent communicators but also good listeners; decisive but reflective; and so on. The idea that we should create the perfect manager has, therefore, (thankfully) been discarded. Organizations now increasingly recognize that the key to success lies, not in trying to develop every skill in every individual, but in accepting that people make varying contributions in group situations and that each of these needs to be developed. This approach is more in line with the central theme of this book; that the need is to recognize and incorporate people's distinctive contributions.

Developing the management team

A major contributor to this change of approach was Meredith Belbin (1981) who, with his colleagues, conducted a study of different management teams in action. His conclusions were that

(a) It was possible to identify and distinguish eight distinct management styles or 'team roles'.

(b) The managers studied tended to adopt one or two of these team roles fairly consistently.

(c) Which role they became associated with was capable of prediction through the use of psychometric tests.

(d) When team roles were combined in certain ways, they helped to produce more effective teams.

(e) Such team roles were not necessarily associated with a person's functional role (e.g. accountant, marketing, etc.) but the way in which they were combined seemed to affect job success.

(f) Managers were more effective when they recognized their own best role and, on the basis of this, tried to make an appropriate contribution to the team (i.e. they recognized and worked on their strengths rather than allowing weaknesses to interfere with their performance).

From his work, Belbin identified eight major roles, as shown in Table 5.1. (This emphasis on roles is similar to Mintzberg's approach.) These are related to the personality and mental ability of individuals and, since each role contributes to a team's success, a successful, balanced team will contain all of them. This is not to say that *all* roles are needed *all* the time – this depends on circumstances – but the team needs *access* to all of them. These roles include the following:

1 *The Chairman* This person coordinates the group and holds the various parts and members together. It is a slightly misleading title for it rather suggests that this person *leads* the group, when this is only true in a limited sense. The Chairman *presides* over the team and is preoccupied with objectives. Chairmen exhibit authority, dominance and discipline but are unlikely to lead the group as regards proposals and strategies.

2 *The Shaper* This is the person who 'shapes' the direction in which the group is going to proceed. (If the Chairman is the 'social leader' of the group, the Shaper is the 'task leader'.) Shapers are apt to be anxious, dominant, extravert, outgoing, impulsive, impatient and often frustrated. They regularly have rows, but they are quickly over and grudges are not harboured. Of all the team, the Shaper is the most prone to paranoia, quick to sense an attack and first to feel a conspiracy. The Shaper exudes self-confidence, which often belies strong self-doubts: only results give reassurance. Shapers may be seen by others as arrogant, abrasive or intolerant; but they make things happen.

3 *The Plant* The Plant is the very dominant, highly intelligent, possibly introverted person who 'scatters seeds' of ideas that others in the group can then cultivate and nourish. They provide the vital spark. The Plant is the team's source of original ideas, suggestions and proposals; plants are the ideas persons. They are far more concerned with major issues, fundamentals and principles than with detail; indeed, they are liable to miss out on details and make careless mistakes. The danger with Plants is that they can devote too much time to ideas that take their fancy rather than falling in with the team's needs and objectives. They may also be bad at taking criticism and be prone to sulk if their ideas are rejected.

Table 5.1 Belbin's team roles

Type	Typical Features	Positive Qualities	Allowable Weaknesses
COMPANY WORKER	Conservative, dutiful and predictable	Organizing ability, practical common sense, hard working self-discipline	Lack of flexibility and unresponsiveness to unproven ideas
CHAIRMAN	Calm, self-controlled and self-confident	A capacity for treating and welcoming all potential contributors on their merits and without prejudice. A strong sense of objectives	No more than ordinary in terms of intellect or creative ability
SHAPER	Highly strung, outgoing and dynamic	Drive and a readiness to challenge inertia, complacency, ineffectiveness or self-deception	Proneness to impatience, irritation and provocation
PLANT	Individualistic, serious-minded, and unorthodox	Genius, imagination, intellect and knowledge	Up in the clouds, inclined to disregard practical details of protocol
RESOURCE INVESTIGATOR	Extraverted, enthusiastic, curious and communicative	A capacity for contacting people and exploring anything new. An ability to respond to challenge	Liable to lose interest once the initial fascination has passed
MONITOR EVALUATOR	Sober, unemotional and prudent	Judgement, discretion and hard-headedness	Lacks inspiration or the ability to motivate others
TEAM WORKER	Socially orientated, rather mild, and sensitive	An ability to respond to people and to situations, and to promote team spirit	Indecisiveness at moments of crises
COMPLETE FINISHER	Painstaking, orderly, anxious and conscientious	A capacity for follow through. Perfectionism	A tendency to worry about nothing. A reluctance to 'let go'

4 *The Monitor Evaluator* This person is also highly intelligent but, unlike the Plant, something of a 'cold fish'. Monitor Evaluators are likely to be serious and not very exciting; creative critics rather than creators. Their contribution lies in measured and dispassionate analysis rather than in creative ideas, and while they are unlikely to come up with original proposals, they are most likely to prevent the team from committing itself to a misguided project. One of their most valuable skills is in assimilating, interpreting and evaluating large volumes of complex written material, and analyzing problems and assessing the judgements and contributions of others. Although Monitor Evaluators are solid and dependable, they lack jollity, warmth, imagination and spontaneity. Nevertheless, they have one indispensable quality; their judgement is hardly ever wrong.

5 *The Company Worker* The Company Worker is the practical organizer; the one who turns decisions and strategies into defined management tasks. The concern of Company Workers is with feasibility and, like the Chairman, they are disciplined and controlled. Company Workers are noted for sincerity, integrity, stability, hard work and trustworthiness but, because they have a continuing need for stable structures, they have a tendency to always try to build them (i.e. a decision will lead to a schedule, a group of people and an objective will produce an organization chart, etc.). They work efficiently, systematically and methodically, but not always flexibly and imaginatively.

6 *The Resource Investigator* Probably the most likeable member of the team: dominant, extravert, sociable and gregarious. Responses tend to be swift, positive and enthusiastic but suggestions and projects can just as quickly be dropped. Resource Investigators are the people who look *outside* the group and acquire information, ideas and contacts. They are a mixture of salesman, diplomat and liaison officer. They are rarely in the office and, when they are, they are usually on the phone. They are quick to see the relevance of new ideas but rarely actually produce them; this is left to the Plant. Within a team Resource Investigators are good improvisers and contributors but if working on their own can easily become bored, demoralized and ineffective. They are not good at 'following up' and, like the Plant, can spend too much time on irrelevances that are of personal interest. But, for all these faults, the Resource Investigator preserves the team from stagnation, fossilization and losing touch with the outside world.

7 *The Team Worker* This is the most sensitive member of the team, the one

who is aware of *others'* needs and is concerned to meet them. The Team Worker is most aware of the emotional undercurrents within the group; most informed about the private lives and family affairs of other members; and the most active communicator. Team Workers are likeable, popular, unassertive, loyal and supportive. They dislike conflict and stand up to the Shaper, Plant or Monitor Evaluator if they feel it is being encouraged. Team Workers are sometimes perceived as soft and indecisive but their support is invaluable to the team and they are certainly missed if they are not there.

8 *The Complete Finisher* As the title implies, this is the team member who ensures that the project is finished. They are anxious, introvert and unassertive – often perceived by others as a 'bit of a pain' for they check every detail and insist that everything is done 'according to the book' – but they galvanize the group into action and keep it focused on deadlines and targets. They are always worried over what might go wrong; are never at ease until they have checked every detail; and can become intolerant and impatient with those who are more casual and slap-happy. The Complete Finisher's preoccupation is order: he/she is a compulsive meeter of deadlines and fulfiller of schedules.

The management matrix

What is interesting about Belbin's work, for our purposes, is that it can be related to the management matrix. I would not want to overstate this, for I

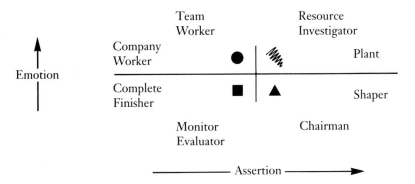

Figure 5.1 Belbin's team members and the management matrix

concede that the fit is better in some instances than others, but I suggest that his eight types can be related to our four cell matrix (Fig. 5.1).

As I say, some of these fit more neatly than others and you may question some of my classifications, but I suggest they can be arranged in this way.

Monitor Evaluators exhibit most of the square characteristics that we talked about earlier. They are sober, prudent, discrete and hard-headed and good at making sure that the project is kept on course and up to schedule. The Complete Finisher, similarly, is painstaking, concerned with detail, conscientious and reliable but perhaps not quite so unemotional. While the Monitor Evaluator makes sure the project tasks are kept on course, the Complete Finisher also makes sure that team members are kept on course. Consequently, I see the former as a square with 'triangular influences' and the latter as a square that is closer to the circle. The weaknesses of Monitor Evaluators are that they tend to lack inspiration and the ability to motivate others while Complete Finishers have a tendency to worry over trivia and a reluctance to let go.

The Chairman appears much more of a triangle. Chairmen's strength is that they are calm, self-controlled and self-confident, able to take a long-term perspective and adopt 'helicopter vision'. They are good at welcoming, incorporating and balancing all contributions. They are certainly more assertive than either the Monitor Evaluator or Complete Finisher but, like the former, are still fairly unemotional. Their organizational ability and eye for detail means that they have some 'square' characteristics. The weakness of the Chairman is that he/she is often no more than ordinary in terms of intellect or creative ability and rather lacks flair – unlike the Shaper, whom I also put in this cell. They too have long-term vision and are keen to get things done, but are less concerned over detail and far more highly strung and emotional. Their dynamism and drive makes them closer to the squiggle and, like the squiggle, they are prone to impatience, irritation and provocation.

The Plant is individualistic and unorthodox (very squiggly features); exhibits considerable flair, imagination, intellect and knowledge; and is often absent-minded and inclined to disregard details of protocol. Plants are certainly assertive, but the fact that they are serious-minded and fairly unemotional means that I have them closer to a triangle than a circle. The squiggle with more circular characteristics is the Resource Investigator, who is outgoing, extravert, enthusiastic, curious and communicative, and possesses the capacity to contact people and explore new opportunities. However, like all good squiggles, Resource Investigators are also prone to lose interest once the initial fascination has passed.

Team Workers appear as circles; socially oriented, keen to support others in their strengths (e.g. building on suggestions) and underpinning members in their shortcomings. In other words, they are very 'group focused'; keen to foster team spirit and improve communications. They are high on emotion (like the squiggle) and, as a result, their weakness is that they can be over-sensitive and indecisive in moments of crisis. But they are very important to the organizational stage of the management cycle.

Company Workers, I feel, are the hardest to place. For convenience I have labelled them as 'a circle with squarish tendencies', but they might equally be considered a 'square with circular tendencies'. They are conservative, dutiful and predictable, and possess considerable organization skills, self-discipline and practical common sense but, in that their orientation is primarily towards the *company* (and its rules and regulations), they are certainly less emotional and people-oriented than the team worker. They are low on assertion – often exhibiting inflexibility, lack of response and sullen acceptance – and, consequently have many similar characteristics to the Plant.

Belbin points out (though he doesn't greatly pursue the point) that those on the right (i.e. higher on assertion) tend to be more 'outward looking' (i.e. focused on the world outside the team) while the four types on the left (lower on assertion) tend to be more inward looking, concerned with issues inside the team. He also points out that different members tend to 'team up' together at different stages in a project. In the initial stages the Chairman links up with the Company Worker to set the project up. Then the Plant makes some proposals and the Monitor Evaluator assesses them. This is followed by the Resource Investigator and Team Worker dealing with people (developing contacts outside the group and generating commitment inside the group respectively) and finally, the Shaper and Complete Finisher are concerned to make sure that the project stays on course and is delivered on time. Notice how, in Fig. 5.1, these pairings involve members from 'opposite sides' of the team. This confirms the point we made in Chapter 2 that opposite shapes can, in certain instances, complement each other.

Belbin's conclusion is that no one individual can possibly combine all qualities but that a team can – and frequently does. It is the group, not the individual, that is the instrument for sustained and enduring success in management. A team can renew and regenerate itself by new recruitment as individual members leave and can find within itself all those conflicting characteristics that cannot possibly be united in any single individual. Moreover, the team must be made up of different types – all too often managers simply pick a team of the cleverest and most talented people and then wonder why it doesn't work. The absence of one role obviously weakens the team, but equally, the presence of *too many* of one type produces predictable kinds of failure. For instance, with too many Plants, good ideas are produced but never taken up; a team composed of Plants and Shapers may look brilliant, but will never deliver; and so on. The analogy of the football team holds: a team made up of eleven strikers or goalkeepers would never beat a well-balanced side.

Many companies now use Belbin's tests to try and determine team membership so that managers can be grouped in work situations where they complement each other. Results show that while some fit very clearly into a particular role, most score high in two or three areas – I score high for Plant, Complete Finisher and Company Worker; not a bad combination for writing a book! – and may even change somewhat over time. (On a later occasion I obtained a much higher score for Monitor Evaluator.) My experience at British Aerospace suggests that many practising managers in a manufacturing setting score high on Company Worker and Shaper. As we noted when discussing our shapes earlier in the book, while some may correspond closely to a particular type others may be more of a mixture. This, of course, helps explain why many groups can operate effectively with less than eight members. What tends to happen is that people may play two roles (their primary role and a secondary one) or, if two team members are competing for a particular role one may 'fill a gap' by switching to play another one. The particular pattern that emerges is, therefore, dependent on circumstances.

6 Negotiation

While managers spend a great deal of their time working in groups of various size, the most common one – and the one that causes managers most concern – is the 'one-to-one-meeting'. This can take many forms and always involves *negotiation*. Managers will meet with many different people in private meetings – colleagues, customers, superiors, subordinates, etc. – for many different purposes, i.e. discipline, grievance, selection, etc. How a manager adjusts his/her style to meet these changing circumstances is a theme of endless management conferences and seminars. Numerous courses are offered on how to deal with difficult people – impossible clients, bosses, colleagues, employees, etc. – and this key question, of how we negotiate with other individuals, is the theme of this chapter.

Assertiveness training

In any course on negotiation skills it is common to find part given over to assertiveness training. The argument usually presented is that the development of assertiveness will assist *any* negotiator in *all* situations but again, I find this too general. It may not be the case that assertive behaviour is appropriate to all circumstances, and managers will certainly vary in the degree of assertiveness that suits their individual personality. Once more, therefore, it is a matter of recognizing individual differences.

Being assertive (as opposed to aggressive or passive/submissive) means being honest with yourself and others. It means having the ability to say directly what it is you want, need or feel, but *not* at the expense of others. Assertion theory is based on the premise that everyone has basic human rights:

(a) The right to refuse requests without feeling guilty or selfish.

(b) The right to consider one's own needs as important as those of others.

(c) The right to express ourselves, so long as we do not violate the rights of others.

Being assertive is *not*:

(a) about getting your own way and winning every time – it is far more about compromise;

(b) a series of quick fix tricks/techniques – the skills have to be learned and practised;

(c) a way of manipulating others – assertiveness is to the benefit of *both* parties.

The rise of assertiveness training can be closely linked with the growth of new groups in the work population (e.g. ethnic minority groups) and the changing role of women. Many feel that these groups have been conditioned, for far too long, to be passive and subservient in the work situation and should be encouraged to stand up more for their basic rights. The argument is that, by being assertive, you are more likely to get more of what you want; you will feel better about yourself and your behaviour; and you will feel better about the other person (Fig. 6.1).

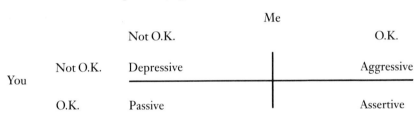

Figure 6.1 The gains from assertive behaviour

There are two particular thoughts that most people are likely to take away from difficult situations:

(a) What actually happened?
(b) How did I handle it?

The point is that while the first may seem more important at the time, it is the second that stays with us longer. For instance, we might experience a poor meal in a restaurant. Some people lose their cool (i.e. act very aggressively) while others say nothing at all (i.e. are passive/submissive). When we look back on the situation we won't remember the poor meal itself so much as how we responded to the situation. Assertiveness training teaches that if we lose our temper (or, conversely, say nothing) then we will probably not feel as good about the situation as if we had spoken up firmly, but courteously, about our concerns. Being assertive makes us feel better about (a) the situation and (b) ourselves.

IDENTIFYING THE BASIC STYLES
There are all sorts of clues which help identify each of the styles.

1   The submissive/passive style
People who are submissive fail to stand up for themselves, and allow their rights to be violated. Their aim is to be safe, to let others take responsibility and to obtain help and sympathy. The basic belief is 'I lose/you win'; 'I'm not okay, you're okay'. The 'body language' of such persons (i.e. the message they convey through their stance, facial expressions, gestures, etc.) will include downcast eyes, the shifting of weight, a slumped body, the wringing of hands, a hesitant/giggly tone of voice and a gentle smile. Such persons may experience fear, anxiety, guilt, depression, fatigue and nervousness and are likely to keep their emotions hidden. The effect on other persons is that it can stir up feelings of guilt, anger or frustration. Others find it hard to disagree without appearing hurtful, unsympathetic or hostile.

2   The aggressive style
People who adopt this style certainly stand up for their rights – but to the point of violating the rights of others. The aim is to be on top; to put others down. The basic belief is 'I win/you lose'; 'I'm okay, you're not okay'. Aggressive people quickly become annoyed, use bullying words and gestures, do not appear to be listening and are prone to lose their temper. As regards body language, characteristics include evenly spread weight, feet planted apart, hands on hips, pointing fist/finger, narrowed glaring eyes, clenched jaw, etc. The effect on others is that it makes them feel frightened, hurt, defensive, humiliated, resentful, under-utilized and dependent. They cannot disagree without being seen as either presumptuous, defensive or incompetent.

3   The assertive style
With the assertive style people stand up for their own rights but do not violate the rights of the other person. The intention is to find out *what* is right, not *who* is right. The basic belief is 'I win/you win'; 'I'm okay, but you could be too'. Assertive people are likely to be firm, but pleasant. They will listen carefully and can take criticism, but will uphold a viewpoint. Body

language characteristics include good eye contact (but not staring) and a comfortable stance. They talk in a strong, steady tone of voice and use phrases like 'let's see', 'what do you think?', etc. They avoid words like 'should' and 'ought'. Their emotions can vary, but they are always kept under control. The effect on others is that they feel in touch, informed and important. People like being around assertive people: they know where they are and can feel confident.

In many situations assertive behaviour is advantageous. This is because it provides the following:

1 *Greater self-confidence*. You achieve success without heated arguments.

2 *You treat others as equals*. You recognize others – their abilities and limitations – rather than regard them as superiors or inferiors.

3 *Greater self-responsibility*. Instead of blaming others (aggressive) or constantly saying 'sorry' (submissive) you take responsibility for your own actions.

4 *Greater self-control*. Your mind is concentrating on the behaviour *you* want: you are not submitting to the control of others.

5 *It can produce 'win-win' situations*. Both people's opinions are given a fair hearing, so both can feel they have won.

THE ASSERTIVENESS PENDULUM

The danger with much assertiveness training, as we noted earlier, is that it suggests assertive behaviour is *always* preferable. The truth is (and many acknowledge this) that there may be times when it is appropriate to be more aggressive (e.g. when your life/property are being threatened) or more passive (e.g. when listening to a lecture). I maintain that an important part of

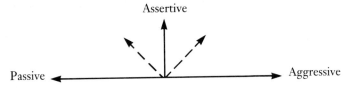

Figure 6.2 The assertiveness pendulum

assertiveness training is learning when to *choose* to assert yourself. In this way, deciding to be more passive/aggressive is a form of manifesting one's own assertiveness. Consequently, I prefer to think in terms of an 'assertiveness pendulum' (Fig. 6.2) which offers a *range* of assertive behaviour: *total* aggression or submissiveness are not advised in any circumstances but assertive behaviour can vary considerably, depending on circumstances.

The key stages for developing assertiveness are, therefore:

1 Recognize your style.

2 Identify situations in which you wish to become assertive.

3 Describe your problem specifically. Indicate who, when, what, how, etc.

4 Devise a script for dealing with the situation.

5 Consider your body language (e.g. eye contact, body posture, clear speech, tone of voice, gestures, etc.)

6 Learn how to listen. Show that you hear/understand. Exhibit empathy for the other person's point of view.

7 Say what you want to happen, but arrive at a workable compromise. There may be limits to how assertive you can be.

8 Avoid manipulation: don't push others (or be pushed yourself) into an unacceptable style.

THE MANAGEMENT MATRIX

Introducing the pendulum offers a more *flexible* approach to assertiveness training: it reminds us that there are not fixed skills that have to be 'learned' but skills that need to be adjusted for different people and situations. Managers need to be constantly amending their style.

On one management course I attended we were asked to think of people we worked with whom we found difficult, and we then had to complete a questionnaire stating whether we considered them more active, less thoughtful, more flamboyant, less disciplined, etc. than ourselves. In all we answered some fifty questions and these were scored to provide certain 'types'. The trainer then suggested these could be located on the grid shown in Fig. 6.3.

A distinction was made between behaviour that was (a) passive or aggressive and (b) people-oriented or task-oriented. This provided four main types – which the trainer labelled Relater, Entertainer, Analyzer and Ruler – and, again, it can be seen that our management matrix (Fig. 2.1) corresponds to this.

The *Analyzer* is very much the square – task-oriented, fairly passive, attentive to detail, concerned to get things right, accurate, organized and reliable. Under pressure Analyzers can become silent, withdrawn or autocratic. What they want above all else is *order*, and the trick in handling such people is to deal with a situation formally in an appropriate setting; discuss it logically and steadily, step by step; use logical facts and provide a clear way forward; and tie in new ideas to old ones. A swift dismissal of the problem will prove counter-productive: Analyzers must be given reasons, explanations and procedures if they are to be effectively motivated.

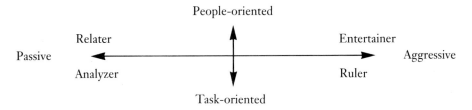

Figure 6.3 Matrix for identifying difficult people

The *Ruler* corresponds to our triangle; task-oriented, but much more assertive. Indeed, Rulers are so focused on completing the task that they may, at times, appear dictatorial. This determination and decisiveness is a great strength but the danger is that the Ruler can easily be perceived as intimidating, which can alienate people. Under pressure they can yell, erupt, throw tantrums and bully and appear exceedingly arrogant. Their overriding need is for *control* and, consequently, the way to deal with them is to recognize their goals; be businesslike and organized; avoid small talk and excessive detail, and get to the point; provide key information and expect a swift decision; and remain focused on the task in hand.

The *Relater* is, of course, our circle – not terribly assertive, and people-focused. Such people are agreeable, loyal, friendly, personable and caring – keen to get along with others. As their overriding need is *harmony*, the way to deal with Relaters is to be casual and sincere; to listen and, if necessary, slow things down; to show you care and exhibit concern; to set clear goals and procedures; and to emphasize self-development.

Finally, the *Entertainer* can be recognized as our squiggle – assertive, outgoing, people-oriented, creative, warm, charming and energetic. The great strength of Entertainers is that they are optimistic, encouraging and persuasive, but their weakness is that they can be egotistical, erratic and disorganized. In that their overriding need is *influence* – to be noticed, applauded and rewarded – the way to deal with them is to enthuse; to let them talk and express their ideas; to use visual demonstrations as opposed to lengthy detailed arguments; to seek out special projects that they might become involved with; and to retain a flexible approach to problems.

How important it is for effective managers to recognize different styles was illustrated by a study in the United States where a group of workers were each asked how they perceived their boss. What was interesting was that nearly all saw their boss as having the same shape as themselves, i.e. squares thought he was a square, circles thought he was a circle, and so on. This tells us a lot about the manager; indeed, it tells us that he was a good one. Let's think about this for a moment. If you are the boss of a firm and you know that Roger the company accountant (an arch square if ever there was one!) is coming to see you first thing on Monday morning, how do you spend your weekend? You know that Roger will arrive with all the facts and figures in immaculate condition so, naturally, you spend the weekend making sure of your facts. The result is that Roger goes back down the corridor happy with the meeting for he feels you are 'like him' and 'on his wavelength'. Alternatively, if Wendy comes to see you – Wendy is a much-loved, long-serving member of the team; a typical circle – you don't dive straight into the profit and loss accounts but spend a few moments talking to her about her family, holidays, interests, etc. This makes Wendy feel you care for her as a person; will encourage her to like you because she feels you like her; and will greatly motivate her at work.

What we are saying is that *general* tenets (e.g. be assertive, be a good listener, be precise, etc.) don't always apply – indeed, they could, depending on the circumstances, prove counter-productive. This is terribly important in an area such as sales. Good salesmen are not just articulate, dominant, informed, enthusiastic and positive. Far more important, they are *flexible*; ready to adjust their approach depending on the customer. The good salesman is, instinctively, 'sussing out' customers and classifying them into particular categories.

I would not wish, however, to overstate this. In responding to the other person I am not suggesting that a manager should *abandon* his/her natural shape. Subordinates may well, in the first instance, welcome a *move* towards their own shape (as we saw above) but eventually they could become frustrated if they felt their superior was just like them. Indeed, they might well start to ask 'Why shouldn't I have their job'? To interact effectively the trick seems to be to move towards the other person's shape initially – a useful tactic might be to move towards an adjacent shape (e.g. a squiggle could become more of a circle or triangle in dealing with a square) – in order to create trust, and then move back to one's original shape once confidence is established. As we noted in Chapter 1, people can, in the *long term*, often work very effectively with people in the opposite cell, for each party can provide complementary skills (as Belbin observed). It is important to remember that you don't necessarily have to *like* people to work well with them (though this may remain important for many circles). Some squares may like to be dominated by squiggles even if it maddens them: they may come to appreciate the other person's qualities and, particularly if this feeling is returned, the relationship can prove effective.

Negotiating skills

The theme of this chapter is that in any form of interaction we are *negotiating*: we're negotiating all the time, whether we like it or not. It is not a specialist activity reserved for industrial relations managers and trade unionists but something that all of us do all the time. The aim, as we have seen, is to obtain 'win-win' situations – in which both parties can feel they have obtained a satisfactory deal – but to achieve this it is necessary to amend one's approach constantly. A key element in doing this is to understand the various 'gambits' (i.e. rituals, conventions, etc.) that operate in the negotiating process. To illustrate the point let's imagine you've seen a car advertised for £1000. You think it's excellent value at that price (and will pay it) but decide to open the bidding at the 'silly' figure of £500. If the other party says 'yes' immediately you are left feeling (a) Could I have done even better? and (b) What's wrong with the car? The problem is that the other party didn't go through the 'gambits'. Had they laughed at the first suggestion, and got you to finally settle at £750 you'd have gone home feeling better even though you'd paid £250 more for the car! The amount itself is not the sole issue: how we feel is equally important.

The gambits themselves can be considered in three phases. There may be others but these are the main ones that are usually identified. The point is that we instinctively use these, and have them used against us, but *how* and *when* depends on circumstances.

(A) Opening gambits
All these gambits are used in the early stages of negotiation and help establish ground rules between the two parties.

1 *Reluctance* Always appear hesitant to buy and, if possible, hesitant to sell. Don't be over eager (as we saw in the case of the car); play 'hard to get'! By seeming to be unenthusiastic about the negotiation you encourage the other side to get you interested. Circles are often poor at this gambit and prone to give in too easily.

2 *The flinch* You should visually react any time a proposal is made to you. (Squiggles and triangles are excellent at this.) People are looking for your response. If you don't react, you indicate that the proposal is not unreasonable, and invite further demands.

3 *Agreement* When you first meet people agree with them (i.e. agree about the weather, etc.). Agreeing with people diffuses their desire to compete. Circles in particular will be put off by a person who doesn't agree with them in the initial stages.

4 *'Want it all'* In the early stages, ask for more than you want. By doing this, you leave room to make concessions to the other side. This promotes 'win-win' negotiation, in which both sides can feel they have accomplished something.

5 *First offer* Never jump at the first offer (as the other person did in our car example). When you say 'yes' to the first offer, people automatically think they could have done better or something is wrong with the proposal. You should go through the processes of negotiating no matter how good the first offer is.

6 *The vice* The vice technique squeezes people with a simple phrase: 'Sorry, you'll have to do better than that'. This technique works because there is usually always more that can be done.

7 *Funny money* Funny money is a way of breaking down the price (or proposal) to make it seem less. Salesmen do this with hire purchase, etc.

(B) Middle gambits
All these gambits, and others, are frequently used in the middle phases of the negotiating process.

1 *Higher authority* This is an indication that a higher authority is needed to make final approval of a deal or to approve changes in the negotiating position (e.g. 'I'll have to clear that with my superior'.) It serves as a way of putting pressure on people without confrontation; moving responsibility for the pressure to some vague entity.

2 *Splitting the difference* Never offer to split the difference in a negotiation, but always try to get the other side to make such an offer. (Triangles are good at this; circles poor.) When the other side offers to split the difference, treat that mid-point as a new offer on their part. You can then work to negotiate an agreement in the range between the mid-point and your position.

3 *Act smart ... play dumb* Generally speaking, act dumb. (Squiggles can be poor at this.) Acting too smart breeds competition. If you act dumb people will drop their guard, be supportive, and go out of their way to help and explain things to you. (This is a particularly good approach with circles.)

4 *The trade off* If someone asks you for something, ask for something in return right away. Don't concede anything, even if the concession means nothing to you. Make a point of the request, so that if you're not able to use the concession right away, you can use it later. (Circles find this hard.)

5 *Set aside* This technique is used when an impasse is reached. It involves setting aside the objection and dealing with other issues. An impasse should not be confused with deadlock, which kills the negotiation. The apparently unresolvable impasses become more flexible after agreement is reached on smaller issues.

6 *Third party* This technique is used when an actual deadlock is reached. Someone who is perceived by both sides as a neutral third party is included to help get past a complete halt in the negotiation. (This approach is common in industrial relations.)

7 *Hot potato* This is when other people want to give you *their* problem. (Circles can be prone to this.) Be careful not to let it become *your* problem, and a distraction from the matter under discussion.

8 *Printed word* Showing people a statement in writing helps support a point. People believe things they see in writing that they won't believe otherwise. (This particularly applies to squares.)

(C) Closing gambits
These are the main gambits that people use to bring the negotiating process to a close. In these closing stages the stakes are considerably higher as both parties will have invested considerable time and energy.

1 *Walk away* Always show that you are prepared to turn down a deal and walk away. (There is a point in the negotiating process when you will not

want to walk away; at this point you are very vulnerable.) Remember that there is nothing you can't live without, so always reserve the right to walk away.

2 *Good guy/bad guy* This technique is often used in police interrogations. One person takes a hard line in the negotiations and is then followed by someone who takes a more conciliatory, friendly line. The aim is for the bad guy to 'soften up' the other person for the good guy. One can use this technique effectively (e.g. with circles) by switching between the two roles.

3 *Withdrawn offer* This is where you withdraw an earlier offer, because you made a mistake perhaps, or a higher authority intervened. If the other side has become committed they may well accept your revised offer in order to save the negotiation. This gambit is effective in drawing negotiations to a close, but you are calling the bluff of the other party and playing for high stakes.

4 *The decoy* This is when an issue is raised that is designed to take your attention away from the real issue. The decoy is then conceded in an effort to get a concession on the real issue. The decoy is a misleading trick – the sort of clever ploy that might be used by a squiggle! Be sure you are negotiating the real issues.

5 *The nibble* After everything has been agreed to, people often ask (successfully) for a little more. This should be obtained fairly easily if the other person has agreed to the overall deal (e.g. 'That price for the car *does* include a new radio doesn't it?').

6 *Puppy dog* This is where one party allows the other to try a product (or whatever) on approval (i.e. It is like the pet shop salesman who lets the little girl have the puppy dog on approval because they are confident she'll never want to bring it back). Many retail stores use this tactic to great effect and build up loyal customers.

7 *Write contract* You should try to be the one to write any contract. The person who writes the contract can write the details in his or her favour, and then it is up to the other person to change them. Squares are good at this.

8 *Easy acceptance* Always put the other person in a position in which they don't feel bad about giving in to you. i.e. Try and create a 'win-win' situation.

In discussing these various gambits I am not suggesting that they are necessarily ethical or even advantageous – merely that they exist and we need to be aware of them. Managers use these gambits continually and they lie at the heart of effective negotiation. Developing management skills is, therefore, largely about learning how to play and counter the various gambits.

CONCLUSION
At the end of the day, the signs of a successful negotiation can be summed up as follows:

1 Both parties can feel they have won.

2 Each seemed concerned about the objectives of the other side.

3 Each side can feel that the other side acted fairly. People don't mind losing so much if they feel the rules were abided by.

4 Each side should feel that it would enjoy dealing with the other person again.

5 Each side should feel that the other will keep the commitments agreed.

To summarize the main points of this chapter; the key quality for a good negotiator is not assertiveness, charm, gift-of-the-gab, knowledge or style – but *flexibility*. This ranks way ahead of the others. The essential requirement is the ability to understand the other person and to be able, appropriately, to move in and out of the various approaches and negotiating gambits. This is particularly important for a manager when dealing with subordinates, for it influences how we lead and motivate people, the topics we move on to in the next two chapters.

7 Leadership

We now enter the third quadrant of the management cycle where we are concerned with leadership and motivating. It is an area where we can expect squiggles to be prominent but other shapes too may find themselves having to lead and motivate in particular circumstances.

Managers consider leadership a very important topic – I receive more requests for courses on 'leadership skills' than almost any other – but, while leadership clearly affects an organization's performance and effectiveness, I have to confess that the more I study the subject, the less convinced I become that one can offer anything terribly definitive on it.

Not that some don't try. A course handbook I acquired recently on leadership read as follows.

What are the characteristics of leadership?

1 A leader knows where he or she is going and is strongly committed to getting there.

2 A leader is able to communicate these goals to his/her followers in such a way as to inspire or motivate them.

3 He or she shows this commitment through unequivocal actions (i.e. He or she 'leads from the front').

4 A leader is able to inspire confidence in his/her followers.

5 A leader mobilizes all necessary resources to achieve the objectives.

6 A successful leader does not need to 'prove' to anyone that he or she is better than they are.

As will become apparent in this chapter, I don't feel these sorts of statements take us very far: I find them bland, vague, simplistic and, in many instances, wrong. It seems to me that when it comes to the teaching of leadership there is a great deal of misunderstanding.

Leading and managing

The first mistake that many make is that they consider leading and managing to be synonymous: leaders have to be managers and managers have to be leaders. This is certainly true to an extent, but only to an extent, and the danger is that we easily overlook the important *differences* between the two.

The problem for managers is that they are invariably both leaders and led at the same time. Even the President of the United States, supposedly the most powerful leader in the world, is constrained by Congress and the Supreme Court! The typical middle manager is constrained from above while trying to lead those below. Indeed, one can say that instructions received from a superior (to manage) invariably conflict with attempts to lead subordinates. Far from being synonymous there is, therefore, a *tension*

Table 7.1 The tensions between leadership and management

The leader	*The manager*
Talks about philosophy	Solves daily problems, makes decisions
Makes contact with employees at all levels	Meets formally with subordinates
Is warm and supportive	Is aloof and critical
Projects key values	Is inconsistent
Concentrates on business strengths	Concentrates on weaknesses
Talks about future goals	Talks about current events
Does not plan to fill his/her diary	Fills his/her diary
Easy to meet	Difficult to meet
Integrates new people	Rarely deliberately meets new people
Anticipates future changes	Little anticipation
Uses intuition and thinks strategically	Does not trust intuition

between leadership and management, as Table 7.1 shows, with the two often pulling against each other.

This is, of course, to overstate the position: as with all stereotype tables, the differences are exaggerated to make the point. In reality, leadership and management are clearly intertwined, but the differences between the two must also be appreciated. The distinction was neatly summed up by Warren Bennis when he said that 'Managing may be "doing things right" but leadership is about "doing the right things"'.

WHAT IS LEADERSHIP?

Having established that leadership is not merely another word for management, are we now in a position to state precisely what it is? Clearly, the term 'leader' implies 'followers' and it also implies people – one cannot lead machines. One might, therefore, define leadership as 'the capacity to mobilize a potential need in a follower'. This means that the minimal conditions for leadership are:

(a) a group of people,

(b) a common task or need,

(c) a division of responsibility within the group.

Over this there is little disagreement: far more contentious is the issue of why some people emerge as leaders while others do not.

Theories on leadership

There have been many different approaches to leadership but I suggest they can be summarized under three main headings – what I term the trait, best style and contingency approaches.

I THE TRAIT APPROACH

This approach suggests that leaders have particular traits (i.e. certain physical, mental or social characteristics) and that you either have what it takes to be a leader, or you don't. The claim is that 'leaders are born, not made'. Numerous studies have been done comparing the physical, intellectual and personality traits of leaders and followers but, while one might accept that, in general, leaders tend to be more intelligent, self-confident, well-adjusted, dominant and extravert, other traits seem far less certain. The argument (put forward by a number of writers) that leaders tend to be physically taller, for instance, hardly seems to hold up when one thinks of Napoleon, Gandhi or Churchill. The problem with the trait approach is that while leadership traits might apply in most instances one doesn't have to look far for exceptions. I remember discussing leadership traits with a colonel at a military college (where the trait approach to leadership training is given considerable prominence) and he showed me the list of traits taught at Dartmouth, West Point, Shrivenham and Cranwell. The interesting thing was that they were all different! There is no set of personality characteristics that has been found to recur in leaders: on the contrary, leaders are noted for being markedly different from each other in terms of personality.

Leadership 'themes'
While remaining somewhat sceptical of the trait approach I would not, however, wish to dismiss it altogether. There are certainly generalizations we can make about leaders and I feel a useful way forward has been offered by Golzen and Garner (1990) who maintain we should avoid talk of 'traits' and 'characteristics' (which are too restrictive) and pay more regard to 'themes'. They claim that there are certain themes (events and experiences rather than traits) that appear common in the lives of successful managerial leaders.

1 *High parental expectations* A noticeable proportion of chief executives in *Who's Who?* are elder sons, and higher expectations are held of older children. Many successful top managers cite parental influence as decisive in a subsequent career.

2 *Early experience of leadership* Many managerial leaders were *previously* elected to leadership positions; at school, in sport, in the community, etc.

3 *Clear and well-communicated objectives* Effective leaders usually have clear objectives and are adept at transmitting these to others. They provide clear plans, a high profile and determination.

4 *Ability to take risks that come off* Successful leaders appear able to analyze a situation; calculate the odds for success; and pick the right issues on which to stand.

5 *Autonomy* Managerial leaders do not need the approval of others. The desire to be liked can be a major barrier to leadership.

6 *Psychological and physical stamina* Leaders can make decisions, stick to them, put up with stress and work long hours. Most managerial leaders are what others would call workaholics.

7 *Ability to pick people* Managerial leaders are good at team-building and delegating. They have a 'helicopter mind' and can see the broad picture. They do not get involved in detail or interfere more than is necessary. They are good at spotting winners among subordinates and letting them get on with it.

8 *Awareness of personal strengths and weaknesses* Managerial leaders are good at appreciating their own weaknesses and skilled at choosing people who can help them.

These themes, in my experience, are common in the lives of successful managerial leaders and I feel this approach is unquestionably preferable to a search for narrowly defined traits.

2 THE 'BEST STYLE' APPROACH

This approach, which largely superseded the trait approach, argues that effective leadership is not dependent on a leader's make-up but on the particular *style* that leaders adopt. We can break these down into two-, three- and four-style approaches.

(a) The two-style approach

Douglas McGregor (1966) distinguishes between two main leadership styles; what he terms Theory X and Theory Y. Theory X, he suggests, is based on the following assumptions:

1 The average human being has an inherent dislike of work and will avoid it if possible. Thus management needs to stress productivity, incentive schemes, 'a fair day's work', etc.

2 Most people must be coerced, controlled, directed, threatened with punishment, etc. if they are to work satisfactorily and not disrupt the organization's aims.

3 The average human being prefers to be directed, wishes to avoid responsibility, has relatively little ambition and wants security above all else.

This attitude (which largely stems from the earlier work of Frederick Taylor) is criticized by McGregor because it leads to an *authoritarian* style of management which is invariably ineffective.

As an alternative, McGregor advocates Theory Y management, which accepts that:

1 The expenditure of physical and mental effort at work is as natural as rest or play. The ordinary person does not dislike work; it depends on the situation.

2 External control and the threat of punishment are not the only means for bringing about effort. People will exercise self-direction and self-control in the service of objectives to which they are committed.

3 Commitment is best obtained by encouraging a feeling of job satisfaction and achievement.

4 The average human being learns, under proper conditions, not only to accept but also to *seek* responsibility.

5 Many more people are able to contribute creatively to the solution of organizational problems than in fact do so.

6 At present the potentialities of the average person are not being fully used.

McGregor's work (which I discuss further in the next chapter) places leadership problems squarely in the lap of management. If employees are lazy, indifferent, uncreative, uncooperative, or whatever then the problem lies with management and their leadership style. The answer lies in adopting Theory Y as opposed to Theory X.

(b) The three-style approach
The two-style approach has been extended by various writers (e.g. Lewin (1951), Baumgartel (1956)) who identify three main styles, one of which is preferable to the others. The terminology varies, but the three groupings are:

Style 1 – Authoritarian, autocratic, dictatorial management – i.e. the leader makes the decision.

Style 2 – Democratic, participative, consultative management – i.e. the group makes the decision.

Style 3 – Laissez-faire, detached management – i.e. each individual decides for him/herself.

The claim is that the democratic style is preferable to the other two but the problem with all these theories is that we cannot determine causality. Does a democratic style lead to an effective team, or does the effective team *permit* the democratic style? There may be circumstances when the alternative styles prove more effective.

(c)   The four-style approach

Finally, Rensis Likert (1961) has subdivided McGregor's X and Y theories into four styles of leadership.

Style 1 – Autocratic (exploitive, authoritative) This assumes that employees are lazy and are only motivated by threats and coercion.

Style 2 – Paternalistic (benevolent, authoritative) An intermediate form: managers still rely on rewards and some coercion, but they genuinely have the interests of employees at heart. The people at the top think of themselves as 'fair but firm' father figures, and employees are treated more like children than adults.

Style 3 – Consultative Leaders consult subordinates before taking decisions.

Style 4 – Participative Employees are involved directly in decision making; this creates greater commitment and a feeling of trust in superiors.

Likert quotes considerable research to support his contention that moving from Style 1 to 4 'results in greater efficiency, production, low wastage and excellent labour relations'. With Style 4, employees see the leader as supportive, friendly, and helpful. They acknowledge that the leader is out to serve their best interests and respond accordingly.

However many styles are identified, the message remains essentially the same; treating people with respect and allowing them to participate in decision making results in more effective leadership. In most instances we might concede that this is true but there are situations, I suggest, where a democratic, participative style is *less* appropriate than, say, the autocratic or laissez-faire. This brings us to the contingency approach.

3   THE CONTINGENCY APPROACH

There has been a move away from the 'best style' approach to one which maintains that effective leadership is that which is appropriate for a particular situation. In other words, it responds to environmental *contingencies* (i.e. changing circumstances). Instead of leaders being 'born' it is now a case of 'cometh the hour, cometh the man'. This is known as the contingency approach and it implies that virtually anyone can be a leader – depending on the circumstances.

Hersey and Blanchard's model

Hersey and Blanchard (1988) have provided a model which suggests there are two categories of behaviour that should be considered when analyzing manager effectiveness:

(a) Relationship behaviour (personal support, encouragement and recognition)

(b) Task behaviour (direction and structure)

These two categories are, of course, similar to those I have introduced in earlier chapters, and they again provide us with four styles of management. Unlike Likert, however, Hersey and Blanchard do not claim that one style is *better* than another – merely different. In their view the different behaviours can be used in differing amounts at different times. Each style is effective when used at the right time and place (Fig. 7.1). The conditions that determine the effectiveness of a style are (a) the group, (b) the task and (c) the organizational environment.

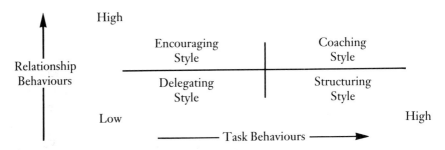

Figure 7.1 Hersey and Blanchard's management grid

   With the *structuring style* the leader largely decides how the task can best be accomplished; communicates clear instructions to the subordinate;and monitors performance. The style is appropriate where people are new to the job, demotivated, insecure or performing below standard, but inappropriate for workers who are skilled, experienced, well-motivated and confident. It is also inappropriate in situations where it is difficult to measure production or where time pressures are not critical.

   The *coaching style* focuses more on interaction: the leader discusses and explains the task and agrees objectives with the subordinate. The aim is to *facilitate* rather than demonstrate. The style is appropriate where subordinates are reasonably skilled and experienced (but may be performing below standard), respect the manager and want to have responsibility. It is least appropriate where workers are very skilled and experienced, highly motivated, do not require the manager's instructions or, conversely, have little skill, experience or confidence.

The main concern of the *encouraging style* is to ensure that subordinates are increasing their confidence and ability; it calls for good interpersonal skills. It is appropriate when managing people who are quite skilled and experienced, self-motivated and performing well and where there are different ways of doing a task. The aim is to create a climate that fosters learning, independence and self-confidence rather than close task supervision. The style is least appropriate when managing people who are not performing up to standard; lack sufficient knowledge, experience and initiative; and do not take responsibility. Misuse of this style can lead to a waste of both human and organizational resources. Some managers may try and create a 'happy family' atmosphere when it is inappropriate.

With the *delegating style* the manager assigns tasks to subordinates and lets them proceed on their own. This is the least interactive style: any manager-subordinate involvement tends to be at a factual, task-related level. This style is appropriate when managing people who possess the required knowledge, skill and experience; are self-confident and highly motivated; take a pride in high quality work; and initiate and accept responsibility. The style is least appropriate when managing people who are new, inexperienced and unskilled; are unwilling to accept responsibility; do not feel comfortable or confident with the task; and are not high standard performers.

Though Hersey and Blanchard are not advocating any particular sequence of styles, and are certainly not suggesting one style is better than another, it seems to me probable that they will be adopted in the order in which we have discussed them and can be viewed in a *progressive* sense in that a manager is likely to move from one style to another as the subordinate matures (i.e. develops skill, experience and motivation). This brings us back to the management matrix – albeit, with the different shapes in different cells (Fig. 7.2).

As we noted, the structuring style is most appropriate with new, insecure, less skilled workers and it is here that a square can be very effective – helping a newcomer to settle in and understand the basics. Because squares are good at detail they are not likely to omit crucial information and will provide effective induction. Moreover, they will not find the newcomer intimidating. Once the worker has started to mature, however, and developed new skills, then a coaching style may be more appropriate and this is where a triangle can prove effective. Like the good football coach the triangle provides clear guidance and instructions and then expects these to be carried out. Only when the worker develops further skills and experience will an encouraging style become appropriate – where the manager befriends the worker; provides considerable autonomy; and offers general encouragement – and at this point circles can prove effective because they are people-oriented.

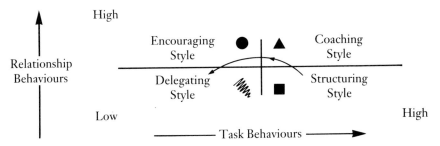

Figure 7.2 The Hersey and Blanchard model revisited

Finally, when the subordinate is so highly skilled and self-motivated that the manager feels he can essentially delegate the job to the worker, a 'squiggly' style of management – in which the manager occasionally makes suggestions, (perhaps for conferences, etc.) and proposes things that the subordinate hasn't thought of – can prove most effective.

The work of Frederick Fiedler
Perhaps the best known contingency writer – though in a sense he also builds on both the trait and 'best style' theories – is Frederick Fiedler (1967). Fiedler believes (like McGregor) that, through questionnaires, people can be divided between those who are 'task-motivated' and those who are 'relationship-motivated'. However, like Hersey and Blanchard, he does not suggest one style is *better* than another; merely that each may be appropriate in particular circumstances (i.e. is contingent upon the situation).

In considering different situations he chooses three *dimensions* by which situations can be thought of as favourable or unfavourable. These are:

(a) leader-member relations – the extent to which the leader feels accepted and supported by group members.

(b) task structure – the extent to which the task is clear and well defined.

(c) leader position power – the power of the leader in relation to the rest of the group.

This allows eight different situations ranging from highly favourable to unfavourable (Fig. 7.3).

Leader-member relations	Good	Good	Good	Good	Poor	Poor	Poor	Poor
Task structure	High	High	Low	Low	High	High	Low	Low
Leader position power	Strong	Weak	Strong	Weak	Strong	Weak	Strong	Weak

Favourable ◄──────── Moderate ────────► Unfavourable

Figure 7.3 Fiedler's range of situations

Fiedler then argues that in very favourable or unfavourable situations – when things are clearly black or white – *task-motivated* leaders seem most effective, while in moderately favourable situations (i.e. 'shades of grey' exist) *relationship-motivated* leaders seem most effective (Fig. 7.4).

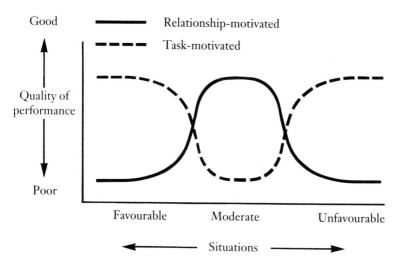

Figure 7.4 Leadership performance in different situations

It should be noted that this is not dissimilar to Thompson's model for decision making which we discussed in Chapter 4. In a highly favourable situation, where it is very clear what needs to be done, the decision making process is a matter of 'calculation' and squares can do this very effectively. Conversely, in a situation where no one is sure what to do (an unfavourable situation for a leader) followers rely on a leader's 'inspiration' to make a decision and see it through. As we noted, squiggles can be effective in this situation.

Situations in between, however – where the leader may be faced with one faction lined up against another – require a more 'relationship-motivated' approach. In such circumstances the leader needs to be less focused on the task and more concerned with holding followers together. This is when circles are more likely to come to the fore.

Like Hersey and Blanchard, Fiedler maintains we cannot speak of 'good' and 'bad' leaders but must consider different leadership patterns in different situations. For instance, an excellent research director may not make a good production manager but this does not mean he/she is a poor leader – merely a poor leader in *that* situation. I believe the contingency approach (which is very much in line with the central theme of my book) provides us with a far more realistic and useful view of leadership. I shall explore it further in the next chapter where we consider how leaders motivate their followers.

8 Motivation

Effective leadership provides good motivation, and motivation is clearly a topic central to management training. If managers are unable to motivate others they will clearly fail and this is why it remains a topic of such interest. Managers are desperate to discover the secret of motivation. In tackling this question, however, we come up against the issue we stated in Chapter 1; to what extent are we all motivated by the same things in the same way and to what extent is each of us unique? Are there 'laws' of motivation or is our understanding of the issue primarily dependent on appreciating how different people 'tick'? The answers to these questions will determine how we approach the topic.

The universal needs approach

In the early part of the century, when managers first became concerned with worker motivation, the widely held view (based on the 'scientific' principles of Frederick Taylor) was that man was basically an 'economic animal'; that if you wanted to motivate him you paid him well and, most important, better than your competitors. Henry Ford, for instance, often boasted of his 'five dollar day' and the fact that he paid his workers over and above his major competitors. Though some might still subscribe to this 'every man has his price' view of motivation today, it is now, however, generally accepted as over-simplistic.

By the middle of the century there was a need for a more sophisticated model of motivation and this was provided in 1943 by Abraham Maslow's 'hierarchy of needs'. Most management courses still start out with a consideration of this, though I have to confess, I am puzzled why this should be. It may be that his approach is so straightforward and appealing, or that it provides a useful starting point from which to introduce later, more effective work, but I have to say that I consider it demonstrably wrong.

Maslow's contention is that as human beings we are faced with a series of needs that can be arranged in hierarchical fashion (Fig. 8.1). We are motivated by these needs and, as one need is satisfied, a higher order need gradually emerges and becomes the motivator for behaviour.

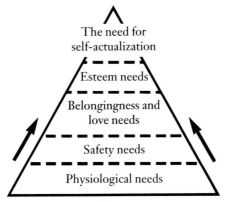

Figure 8.1 Maslow's hierarchy of needs

Man must first of all meet his body requirements: if he is lacking food and water he will only be motivated to seek for them and will not think about other needs. Sadly, for millions in the Third World, this is their overriding concern but those of us in the well-fed Western world all too often take our food for granted. When our first need is met we become less aware of it and the second need in the hierarchy emerges. Man's dominating goal is now a need for safety; everything else seems less important. Consequently man makes weapons, builds houses, creates laws, etc. and if we can reach a point where we feel fairly 'safe', most of the time – from wild animals, climatic conditions, criminal assault or whatever – then other needs start to emerge. Once man feels fed and safe he starts to feel the need for family and friends which in turn creates a need for self-esteem (i.e. he doesn't just wish to mix with other people but wants to feel that others wish to meet him). Finally, if all needs are met this provides a foundation from which man is motivated to develop his 'actual self' – his interests, talents, skills etc.

This is often termed 'content theory' because it adopts a 'package approach', is a universal theory that applies to everyone (with possible minor exceptions), and plays down individual choice and social influence. Maslow implies that everyone must move through these set stages (though writers have debated over the flexibility of Maslow's model) if they are to be fully motivated but he is not suggesting one need has to be satisfied 100 per cent before another can emerge. (For instance, we do not need to be bloated before we feel a need for safety.) In practice, most people are partially satisfied and partially unsatisfied in their basic needs at the same time. A more realistic description would be in terms of decreasing percentages of satisfaction as we go up the need hierarchy. Most of us might meet, say, 85 per cent of our physiological needs, 70 per cent of our safety needs, 50 per cent of our love needs, 40 per cent of our self-esteem needs and 10 per cent of self-actualization needs. Maslow also stresses that the top two layers of his hierarchy can never be fully satisfied.

Maslow's model is unquestionably seductive and, as we shall see, has had a considerable impact on the psychology of work, but it seems to me to be open to considerable attack. The major criticism is that, as a universal theory, it fails to deal with the 'starving artist syndrome'. It presents a harmonious view of life (perhaps reflecting Maslow's middle class, American values) and rather suggests that one is motivated when 'everything in the garden is rosy'. The truth, however, is that many people are motivated in the higher levels when they are *failing* to fully meet their lower needs.

A great creative artist like Vincent Van Gogh illustrates the point. He certainly viewed his life, and most other people did, as a total failure and towards the end of his tragic, short life, when he was living in Arles in the south of France, he was certainly not meeting his basic needs. He was in a wretched state and was committed to an asylum on various occasions. He was certainly not safe from the local townspeople, who wanted him removed from the town, or even from himself when, in a fit of madness he tried to cut off his own ear. He failed to form successful relationships with women; rowed with Gauguin; and never formed any true friendships during his life with the exception of his brother, Theo. Everyone laughed at his 'silly paintings' which worsened his own self-image and, eventually, in 1890, he took his own life. And yet it was during this time, when his lower level needs were manifestly not being met, that he was *motivated* to produce works of art, now recognized as among the world's finest. One could similarly mention Beethoven, who was able to write some of his greatest music when deaf, or cite the numerous literary masterpieces that have been produced in prison. A universal theory of motivation should address these issues and, in that we attack Maslow, we inevitably criticize those who build on his ideas.

MASLOW'S INFLUENCE ON THE PSYCHOLOGY OF WORK

For all its shortcomings, however, Maslow's work has been enormously influential in the psychology of work. His model has spawned a whole group of writers who, collectively, are known as the 'neo-human relations school'. This includes, most notably, Frederick Herzberg, Douglas McGregor,

Renesis Likert and Chris Argyris. Though each presents a particular emphasis and uses different terminology they are all saying essentially the same thing: that specific needs must be met if workers are to be motivated in the work situation. Rather than cover every writer in detail I shall focus mainly on Frederick Herzberg's (1968) motivation-hygiene theory for it has proved enormously attractive to managers and become, as a consequence, highly influential.

HERZBERG'S MOTIVATION-HYGIENE THEORY

Herzberg, in a famous study in Pittsburgh, Pennsylvania, interviewed 200 engineers and accountants and asked them to recall occasions when they felt (a) satisfied and (b) dissatisfied about their work. They were asked how these feelings affected their performance, personal relationships and well-being. Herzberg's central finding was that the factors which alleviated job *dissatisfaction* were different from those which resulted in positive job *satisfaction* and, therefore, these should not be seen as opposite ends of a single continuum but as two separate traits, i.e. the opposite of satisfaction is not dissatisfaction but *no* satisfaction. The factors that related to job satisfaction he termed the 'motivation factors' while those relating to job dissatisfaction he labelled 'hygiene factors'.

(a) Motivation factors – achievement, recognition, work itself, responsibility and advancement.

(b) Hygiene factors – company policy and administration, supervision, salary scales, interpersonal relations and working conditions.

Herzberg claims that the essential difference between the two sets of factors is that the motivators relate very much to the individual concerned – one's own sense of achievement, recognition, responsibility, etc. – while the hygiene factors reflect more the *context* within which one works. Herzberg's contention is that management can do much to improve the hygiene factors (and thereby remove dissatisfaction) by enhancing the work environment, but that this *in itself* can never provide positive motivation. Improving the environment will only further reduce dissatisfaction, but to motivate workers managers must 'enrich' workers' jobs and try and provide them, as individuals, with a sense of achievement, recognition and responsibility.

Herzberg's message becomes clearer if we revert to Maslow's hierarchy of needs (Fig. 8.2). Herzberg concedes that managers have done much to help meet workers' basic needs: canteens and toilets are provided to meet physiological needs; fire escapes, safety regulations and first aid rooms help meet safety needs; while football teams, Christmas parties and tea-breaks help meet belongingness and love needs. But all too often this is where it stops. Management seems to think that by providing *more* of these it will enhance motivation, but Herzberg argues this is not so. Such measures will further improve the hygiene factors, but to *motivate* people – and allow them to move up into the higher levels of Maslow's hierarchy where they can obtain a feeling of self-esteem and self-actualization – one must focus on the motivation factors. One can see why Herzberg uses the terms motivation and hygiene: if you have a hygienic kitchen it may stop your getting ill, but it cannot make you well. To do this *you as an individual* have to be motivated to do something (i.e. give up smoking, get fit, go on a diet, etc.).

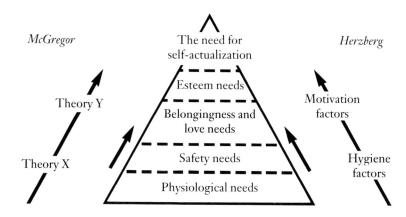

Figure 8.2 The impact of Maslow's hierarchy of needs

Herzberg's work is very similar to McGregor's, which we discussed in the previous chapter. McGregor claimed that too many managers think in Tayloristic terms (Theory X), driving and coercing subordinates rather than encouraging and praising them (Theory Y). He claims that Theory X fails to recognize that man is a wanting animal and that while modern industry may have largely satisfied needs 1 to 3 in Maslow's hierarchy it has done little to develop 4 and 5. Managers need to provide incentives *on* the job so that self-fulfilment can develop. Or, as Argyris puts it, industrial organizations are suited to the capacities and characteristics of the child rather than the adult. The challenge for management is to create work environments in which everyone has the opportunity to grow and mature as an individual. One can see why such writers are labelled 'the neo-human relations school'; their views draw strongly on the Hawthorne studies and the work of Elton Mayo.

CRITIQUE OF THE CONTENT THEORISTS

The critical accounts of Herzberg and McGregor are numerous (see, for instance, Little and Warr (1971)) and I do not wish to spend time regurgitating them in detail; suffice it to say that further studies find their work wanting on a number of counts.

In the first place, evidence suggests that job enrichment schemes are more readily applicable to more highly skilled jobs – it is significant that Herzberg did his studies among engineers and accountants – than to routine, repetitive work. Job enrichment is notoriously difficult to introduce where piece-work is in operation and can all too often end up as job rotation or job enlargement.

Secondly, job enrichment schemes can create problems for trade unions if workers are asked to take over managerial functions, for this could lead to demands for higher pay if workers have greater responsibility. As such schemes involve channelling responsibility down the organizational hierarchy this can also threaten first-line supervisors' jobs, and they will certainly be hampered if they do not receive the support of *all* levels of management.

Finally, and most important, there is evidence that many workers have an 'instrumental' view of work (i.e. they see it as providing income that can then be spent on leisure-time activities) and do not aspire to the higher levels of Maslow's hierarchy. They do not go to work *expecting* it to be satisfying and, therefore, do not seek out responsibility, advancement or recognition. Those with authoritarian personalities (squares?) may actually *prefer* a situation of dependence on, and domination by, others. Because of their instrumental orientation, workers may be reluctant to support attempts to make work more interesting if that necessitates even a short-term cut in production and thereby wages. One might well find cultural resistance to job enrichment schemes: the worker as consumer may be in conflict with the worker as producer and the instrumental concerns may well win out.

Nor is it true that workers in highly specialized, repetitive jobs are *necessarily* bored by them. Baldamus (1961) has shown how workers often develop 'traction' – a feeling of being pulled along by the rhythm of a particular activity. Many appreciate the safety of not being allowed to take decisions and prefer repetition and specified work to change and variety. Herzberg rarely considers differences in intelligence, age, sex, etc. and fails to place the nature of job content into any social or economic framework. A change at work could, in reality, increase both satisfaction and dissatisfaction at the same time. For instance, being offered advancement (a key motivator) might increase our self-actualization, but if it worsened interpersonal relations in the office (because no one thought we were worthy of it) then it would, simultaneously, worsen the hygiene factors.

One can see why Herzberg and McGregor are so popular; their message to management is very simple. The solutions to motivational problems are in *their* hands and by focusing on the design of individuals' jobs and developing job enrichment schemes managers can assist workers attain self-actualization. But isn't the Herzberg model much what we would expect anyway? When things are going well we tend to refer to ourselves; when they are going badly we blame others. Such an approach appears far too simplistic as a model for understanding human behaviour.

Extending Maslow

So far I have largely rejected Maslow's arguments. But one cannot deny their attraction, not just because of their simplicity, but because we can identify with the points he makes and suspect that there is 'something in them'. We are left with the feeling that there might be a grain of truth in what he says and, consequently, are wary of 'losing the baby with the bathwater'. John Hunt suggests that if we amend the terminology – and focus on goals (which are cognitive) rather than needs (which are instinctive) – then there is some justification for the suggestion that people do develop different goals (depending on childhood, socialization, etc.) and that these will affect personal motivation. He suggests eight main goals – comfort, structure, relationships, recognition, power, autonomy, creativity and individual growth (which are not so different from Maslow's needs) – but argues that they vary from one person to another and *do not build on one another in a set order*. In other words, Hunt extends Maslow's needs (relabelling them goals) but rejects his suggestion that they form a hierarchy. Hunt maintains that goals are not static but shift over time in individuals and between individuals within a culture. He also sees the whole process as an individual and cognitive one rather than a universal and instinctive one. A brief discussion will help illustrate Hunt's argument.

Comfort goals are best summarized as a 'comfortable life style'. A person who is strongly influenced by these goals may *seek* a job offering repetitive tasks, regular money and low stress – it is a common pattern among process workers – while a 'high achiever' (in a career sense) will usually rate such goals as a low priority. Comfort goals are likely to be particularly high during a person's teenage years (i.e. when the teenager is keen to obtain money), when a first child is born and in retirement.

Similarly, some people exhibit a strong need for structure goals (i.e. the goal of reducing uncertainty). These are people who have a strong desire to work in a highly structured setting and are attracted to occupations such as the armed services, banking, insurance companies and large bureaucracies. Moreover, Hunt suggests that such people are more likely to be first or only children, to have had over-anxious parents, to be of lower socio-economic status and to have been insecure and deprived in childhood. Such a picture approximates to the square we described previously. The structure goals are closely linked to the comfort goals and together they mirror Maslow's physiological and safety needs. But Hunt's point is that they appear to varying degrees in different people and, rather than evaporating once they have been met, can *re-emerge* at different points in the life cycle.

The relationship goals correspond to Maslow's belongingness and love needs but, again, Hunt insists that some people have a much stronger desire for them than others. Some people will seek out employment that offers the opportunity to form lasting relationships (e.g. nursing, social work, personnel, teaching, etc.) but most high achievers would not. Such people could well be later children from a large, affectionate family; have a strong and persistent pattern of close school-friends; interact frequently in social and friendship groups; and seem to correspond closely to our circle shape. As with comfort goals, relationship goals are more likely to be strong during the teenage years, at the birth of the first child and in retirement.

The recognition goals reflect a desire for recognition from others as well as a desire to manage and control others and, along with power, correspond to Maslow's need for esteem. Hunt, however, particularly focuses on power and suggests that this is the goal most prominent in successful, aspiring managers. (Less successful managers play down power and lay greater stress on comfort, structure and relationships.) People with strong power goals have a wish to affect other people's behaviour, even without their consent. This type of person is likely to have a power figure as a role model (e.g. parent, teacher, coach, etc.); to be confident, ambitious and competitive; and to be a first child in the family. This picture conforms to the triangle.

Finally, the goals of autonomy, creativity and growth correspond to Maslow's need for self-actualization. What Hunt points out, however, is that some may pursue autonomy *along with* creativity, while others pursue them apart. If we consider this in a matrix (Fig. 8.3) we see that different people are attracted to particular jobs and that, once more, the management matrix corresponds to this.

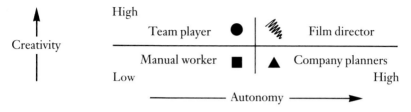

Figure 8.3

Occupations where both autonomy and creativity are high would include film directors, writers, artists, etc. which, I suggest, come close to the creative image we drew of the squiggle. Good team players (e.g. social workers, clerical workers, etc.) wish to be creative but have little need for autonomy. On the contrary, they desire other people's company and are good examples of circles. Some workers (e.g. manual, routine clerical workers, etc.) exhibit low goals for both creativity and autonomy (probably as a result of socialization) and can be labelled squares, while people who do not aspire to be particularly creative but wish to retain their autonomy (such as company planners) are triangles.

This leads us to the point that goals can often conflict with each other and produce much of the stress we experience: career versus family, structure versus risk, autonomy versus team-work, etc. Of all these conflicts, Hunt suggests the two most common are

(1) Relationship goals versus autonomy goals, and

(2) Structure/security goals versus power goals.

If we run these against each other we see that the situation fits the management matrix (Fig. 8.4). Relationship goals (valued by circles) clash with the goal of autonomy (important to triangles). While circles may want to mix with others, triangles have a need to be on their own. Similarly, a need for structure (important to squares) pulls against the need for power (valued by squiggles): the square may seek security which clashes with the squiggle's eagerness for risk taking.

I am highlighting here the tension we observed in Chapter 1, between circles and triangles on the one hand and squares and squiggles on the other.

For Hunt, therefore, motivation is about trying to match the goals of individuals with those of the organization. The problem is that, too often, manager and subordinate fail to recognize that they are different. Power-hungry, loner, career-motivated managers try to design jobs for people who

Relationships   ●   squiggle   Power

Structure   ■   ▲   Autonomy

Figure 8.4

are motivated by goals other than career. They cannot understand why workers seem more interested in meeting friends in the pub than in pursuing their careers. Similarly, workers cannot understand why the manager is such a workaholic. Consequently, both parties end up talking past each other.

The expectancy approach to motivation

Hunt's work moves us neatly away from Maslow (without abandoning him altogether) towards a view of motivation that lays greater emphasis upon individual differences. We are still categorizing but now talking of trends, patterns and themes rather than a universal theory of motivation. No longer are we suggesting that everyone is motivated in the same way – through an ascending hierarchy of needs – but that each individual has a separate set of goals based on personal *expectations*. Expectancy theory (which includes the work of Lewin, Tolman, Porter and Lawler, Vroom, etc.) adopts a cognitive approach and views motivation as a *process*. Individuals are seen as thinking, reasoning beings who have beliefs and expectations about events in their lives and have preferences as to possible outcomes. Expectancy theory can best be explained in terms of a simple diagram (Fig. 8.5).

Expectancy theory can be stated in the form of an equation. If F equals the 'force' of an individual's motivation to behave in a particular way, then $F = E \times V$ where E represents the expectation that the behaviour will be followed by a particular outcome and V the valence (or desire) for the particular outcome. As can be seen from Fig. 8.5, expectation can take two forms, involving the relationship between effort and performance and performance and reward.

We can explain the formula by adding some numbers. For instance, if E (in whatever form) is zero then motivation (F) will be zero however great the desire (V) might be. Similarly, even if the expectation (E) is 100 per cent certain of success then motivation (F) will still be zero if the desire (V) is zero. These two situations can be shown mathematically as $E(0) \times V(1) = F (0)$ and $E(1) \times V(0) = F(0)$.

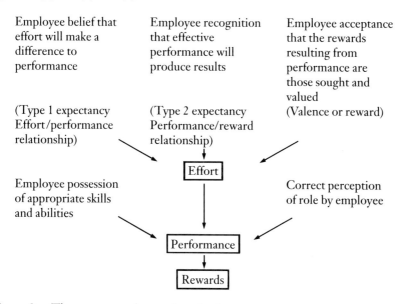

Figure 8.5 The expectancy theory of motivation

We can illustrate with three examples. If you desire promotion (V) but believe that, however hard you try, your effort will not result in satisfactory performance (type 1 expectancy) then you will not be motivated (F). Similarly, if you desire promotion (V) but believe that, however well you perform you will not be rewarded (type 2 expectancy) then you will not be motivated (F). Conversely, if you expect that effort will lead to satisfactory performance (type 1 expectancy) and that performance will result in rewards (type 2 expectancy) you will still not be motivated if you have no desire whatsover (V) to achieve these goals. Therefore, only when both E and V are positive will motivation exist. The extent to which they are positive will determine the effort (Fig. 8.5) and this, along with individuals' skills, and the way they perceive their roles, will affect performance and, ultimately, rewards.

This brings us to the opposite end of the spectrum from Maslow: instead of satisfaction (of needs) leading to performance, as Maslow suggests, it is now performance (based on expectations and desires) that leads to satisfaction. Even the receipt of rewards alone will not result in satisfaction, for this will be determined by the gap between the rewards actually received and *perceived* equitable rewards. For instance, if you *expect* to be paid £200 for a job and you are only paid £150 then you will not feel satisfied. This in turn will have a feedback effect on future desires and expectations.

Expectancy theory sees motivation as a dynamic process; it attempts to measure levels of motivation; it focuses on individuals' varied and changing expectations; and it considers the strength of different valences. Though complex – and I do not suggest in a short discussion that I have provided more than a bare outline – it provides, in my view, a more realistic and fertile approach to motivation. It reminds us that attempts to improve 'satisfaction' may not lead to improved performance because people have different goals. Triangles may want promotion, squares security, squiggles excitement and circles companionship. Motivation is, therefore, a subtle task and reward systems, management styles and organizational structures need to reflect that subtlety.

9   Time management

We now move into the final stage of the management cycle and consider how managers control and monitor their various activities. This is territory where squares feel at home, and probably think they excel but, as we shall see, they often exhibit shortcomings – as, indeed, do the other shapes. A topic that forms a key part of this (and has become increasingly popular on management training courses) is 'time management' – for managers know that they cannot expect to control a working situation if they cannot control themselves – and this is the concern of this chapter. Many managers know that time management is something they do badly and see considerable benefits in becoming proficient at it.

The problem is, however – as with so many of the other issues we have discussed – that managers are once more looking for, and expecting, simple, straightforward answers to what is a highly complex question. Some textbooks and courses offer simple answers but, again, I find these misleading. There are no 'universal truths' on time management.

The basics of time management

It is important to realize that our attitudes to time (and work) are not fixed but are *culturally* determined. There is nothing 'natural' about working 'nine to five', five days a week, forty five weeks a year, or whatever. The ancient Greeks, for instance, believed that work was bad for you and brutalized the mind (which is why slaves were used for heavy labour) and that one's time could be used more effectively in philosophy, the arts, relaxation, etc. And just as different societies can vary in their attitudes to time and work, so can different individuals. It is important to recognize that time management is a very personal thing – though to read some of the textbooks you wouldn't think so.

These textbooks worry me on a number of counts. In the first place they often read like 'kill-joys'. I have read books that provide morbid self-assessment tests which ask you to examine whether you spend too much time watching TV, chatting to friends, drinking socially, etc. and then suggest that you greatly reduce, if not eliminate these. Some even advocate finding ways in which we can maybe take more work home or on holiday! The truth is that we are all bound by the 168-hour limit. We may vary as regards our wealth, talents, energy, etc. but we all share 168 hours a week; no more, no less. Most texts agree that this can be divided roughly as indicated in Fig. 9.1.

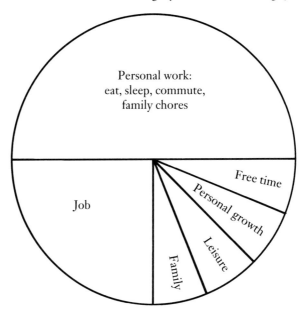

Figure 9.1 How we use our 168 hours per week

This means that approximately 50 per cent of our time is spent on personal activities, 25 per cent on leisure activities and 25 per cent on our job. The trick is not to try and spend more time at work at the expense of other activities – on the contrary, these are important and must be retained – but the work 'quarter' should be used to maximum effect. I would maintain that watching TV, chatting, strolling, window-gazing, etc. are important – for different people to varying degrees – and should be preserved. Chatting to people or dealing with interruptions at work, for instance, are not necessarily 'time robbers' but, in many cases, provide important vehicles whereby certain people become more involved in, and committed to, their work. In fact, interruptions and disjointed conversations are effective and efficient ways of collecting data, and managers should not be advised otherwise.

A second concern, which follows from this, is that many textbooks appear to be written by people who themselves have never worked in industry. One comes across checklists which suggest that you should 'close the door to your office more often' – which isn't much help if you work in an open plan office! Or again, 'delegate more to your secretary' is of little use if you don't have one. Similarly, suggestions like 'reduce your working hours', 'find time to meditate', 'make time for personal relaxation at work', 'have a showdown with your boss', 'look for another job' may be equally unrealistic. They may apply to some but for most they simply produce a guffaw.

Thirdly, textbooks invariably offer a whole range of techniques – time logs, diaries, must-do lists, action plans, etc. – which, if one completed them, would leave little time for anything else! The 'time management techniques' that the purists produce usually fill me with horror. True, there are certain basic principles which can certainly help the practising manager become more effective. There is clearly need for commitment, analysis, planning and re-analysis – for managers to adopt the 'three Rs of time management'; recording, reviewing, revising – but too often this is presented as a set list of guidelines with little reference to the personal differences of each individual. This is why so many managers return from time management courses dispirited by the whole exercise and claiming that 'it didn't apply to them'. The key point is that time management is *not* a panacea – the answer to every manager's problems. It merely provides a set of good habits which, everything else being equal, will assist managers in their daily work. To take an analogy from medicine: I can assure you that you will be less likely to suffer a heart attack if you give up smoking, improve your diet and take exercise, but I cannot *guarantee* that you will not get one. To repeat; we are, like the doctor, in the business of diagnosis rather than prediction.

The time management grid

Many writers talk of a 'time management grid' which is a useful way of moving to a more personalized view of time management. There are three main ways in which managers' time gets used up at work:

(a) Responding to demands from others.

(b) Doing things out of habit – 'routines' that are done automatically. (Good habits provide discipline and structure; bad habits are time-consuming and can blind us to alternatives.)

(c) Making decisions and prioritizing alternatives.

These activities – which correspond to what Rosemary Stewart (1975) has termed the demands, constraints and choices of management – require managers to consider what they *must* do, what they *ought* to do and what they *would like* to do, and to prioritize the alternatives.

Whether something is 'top priority' is determined by two key factors, (a) importance and (b) urgency, and this enables us to construct the grid, containing four types of response (Fig. 9.2). These four labels were used on a course I once attended, but one could easily devise alternatives. I shall consider each in turn, starting with the Dynamo.

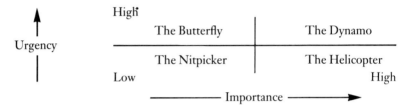

Figure 9.2 The time management grid

(a) *The Dynamo* When a task is urgent *and* important it is likely to be done, but the danger is that it may not be done well. This is the 'crisis cell' and good time managers try to prevent activities falling into this cell if possible. A manager who spends a lot of time in this cell may be energetic and active, but is not well organized.

(b) *The Helicopter* A manager in this cell has the ability to rise above issues and 'take a long-term view' but the danger is that tasks may not get done. Though important, the deadline may be a long way off (or may not exist at all) and, consequently, any decision/action may be postponed. Good time managers, however, spend a lot of time on these tasks for this is the 'planning cell'. The effective manager adopts 'helicopter vision' and can foresee what is likely to happen. Less proficient managers find activities in this cell suddenly spill over into cell (a) and become crises.

(c) *The Butterfly* tends to get things done, because they are urgent, but the danger is that too much time is spent on them. We can easily kid ourselves that these activities are more important than they really are. These jobs should be done quickly; this is the 'quick and simple cell'.

(d) *The Nitpicker* Activities in this cell are neither urgent nor important but the danger for some managers is that they spend too much time on them because they are often easy and/or enjoyable. Nitpickers are at home with familiar detail and the danger is that they become immersed in it. A common problem for many of us is that we tend to start the day with these activities but we get 'sucked into them' as they prove more difficult and/or interesting than expected, and we use up energy that should be reserved for more important tasks. This can easily become the 'time-wasting cell'.

All managers will find themselves in each cell from time to time but the interesting question is which one they gravitate towards. Some managers always seem obsessed with detail; others appear faced with endless crises; others jump from one task to another without ever satisfactorily completing any. What we discover is that, once again, our management matrix corresponds to the time management grid I have just described. Squiggles are 'dynamic' – full of energy and anxious to address the big issues – but the danger is that they indulge too often in 'crisis management'. They are likely to claim that they thrive on crises because it makes them feel important, gets them motivated, creates excitement and provides a feeling of achievement, but it can't be used constantly. The danger with such people is that they all too often *allow* events to slip into the crisis square when they shouldn't. They are often unreliable as regards timekeeping; they are poor at paper work; their desk is probably a mess; and they are erratic and unpredictable in their decisions. Though they may thrive on firefighting and facing 'big issues' this style of management often results in stress and mistakes and proves extremely frustrating for those working with them.

Triangles, on the other hand, are strong on planning, are good at adopting long-term vision, and find time for the 'planning cell'. Time management is likely to be one of their strengths for they are usually effective at prioritizing activities. They are adept at adequately handling the day-to-day issues while keeping an eye on long-term developments.

Circles – because people are important to them and they are keen to please others – are often poor at saying 'no' and prone to respond too readily to the demands of others. They are likely to jump from one thing to another, like butterflies, in an attempt to please all parties, when the tasks may not be that important. They may be urgent to the person making the request and the circle may, mistakenly, think they are also important, but the danger is that circles will become overburdened with other people's trivia.

Talking of trivia, this is also the square's problem. In many ways squares are good at time management; indeed, the problem is that they are *too good* and have difficulty retaining sufficient flexibility. Being cautious, conservative and meticulous, squares are the sorts of people who have very firm work procedures and are highly disciplined, but the problem is that they have difficulty adjusting to change. Squares are so used to the mechanics of specific tasks and to obtaining a high degree of accuracy – for it is more important that tasks are done correctly than done well – that they find difficulty moving to more important and urgent matters that might come along. Squares will stick with old procedures and ancient forms of technology because they are comfortable with them even though superior ways of doing tasks may now be available. While circles may not say 'no' enough, the danger for squares is that they say 'no' too often. This can prove frustrating for managers senior to them, and time management training might even intensify the situation. Ironically, therefore, though the final, control quadrant is favourable territory for squares, they are not always as good at time management as they might like to think!

Delegation

A key part of time management is delegation – for the more effectively we delegate to others the more we release time to spend on the important, long-term issues. If management is about getting things done through people then delegation is a vital ingredient in this. Delegation

* allows people to grow with the job and demonstrate ability;
* gives people a wider and more varied experience of work;
* helps people to feel more involved and trusted at work;
* enables people to find out more about what is going on.

It also provides considerable benefits to the manager.

* It allows the manager to shed certain tasks.
* It develops trust with subordinates.
* It exhibits self-confidence.
* It releases the manager to take on tasks for superiors.

It isn't necessary for managers to be able to do *every* job better than each member of a workteam but they should try and spot those areas of work where others can perform better than them. Areas for effective delegation include:

1 Tasks that others can perform better, e.g. highly technical tasks.

2 Less important work – leaving more time for more important tasks.

3 Routine tasks which can be clearly understood by others. (NB: Tasks that are routine to the manager may be 'something new' to the worker.)

4 Jobs where the workteam has easier access to information (e.g. long-term, ongoing tasks).

If effective communication and good information lead to better decision making then it is effective delegation that often allows this to happen. Delegation is the artery through which the blood of information can flow. If information is not passed down through the organization the artery will become blocked. The manager, therefore, is at the centre of a network of communication with information flowing in all directions.

Curiously, however, delegation is a skill in which we receive little instruction. At school, indeed, it is positively discouraged. If, for instance, I am good at maths but poor at languages I am not allowed to delegate the languages to someone who is good at it (in exchange for their maths) even though this may appear a suitable arrangement. The educational system encourages us to work on our own. No wonder so many managers are poor, and remain poor, at delegation.

A key point to make is that delegation is not simply a technical skill (passing on expertise, etc.) but also a *human* skill. It is an *art*, not a science; a matter of touch rather than firm rules. It is not simply 'passing the buck' but giving someone else

(a) *responsibility* to act on your behalf

(b) the *authority* needed to get the job done

(c) the *resources* (e.g. equipment, finance and people) to get the job done.

An essential point is that while authority can be delegated, *overall responsibility* is not. This is the difference between *relinquishing* a job and delegating it, and the reason why so many are loath to delegate.

THE PROBLEMS OF DELEGATION

In simple terms there are three main problems of delegation: upward delegation, over-delegation and under-delegation. Different people are prone to these and we shall consider each in turn.

Upward delegation

On occasions, subordinates may approach managers and ask them to do the job for them – probably accompanying the request with a complimentary phrase like 'I know you can do it so much better than I'. Such 'upward delegation' is highly flattering, and the manager may well be tempted to do the job, but this reaction is fraught with dangers because

1 The manager has collected a job that is not his/hers to do: the 'tail is wagging the dog'.

2 If managers are doing someone else's job then they are not doing their own.

3 If they allow it to happen once, they may be asked to do it again.

4 They may not be in control of their workteam, as the team appears to be dictating to them what they should do.

5 The worker does not learn to do the job.

Circles and squares are particularly prone to this. Circles will be happy to be approached and keen to maintain good relations with subordinates. They will almost certainly rationalize their action by claiming that it is a way of motivating a worker and showing that, as bosses, they are approachable. Squares too are likely to encourage upward delegation, but for different reasons. They are flattered by the approach because they are recognized for their technical experience and expertise. They probably enjoy doing the task, know they can do it well, and enjoy showing off in front of the subordinate. It could well be a job that they did previously and, quite possibly, one they were happier doing before they took on the exasperating task of managing people. Any opportunity to revert to a previous task is welcomed; but it is often poor use of the manager's time.

Under-delegation
A common danger for managers is that they prefer to do the specialist work for which they were trained rather than concentrate on the supervisory activities of planning, organizing, motivating and controlling others. They fail to pass enough responsibility down the line; try to do too much themselves; and insufficiently involve end-users. There are a number of reasons why many managers are poor at delegating to others:

1 Fear of losing reputation. The manager is afraid it will look as if he/she cannot do the job.

2 Fear of being replaced by someone else, who is seen to do the job better.

3 Lack of confidence in others. The manager fears that subordinates are incompetent and doesn't trust them. They will certainly *become* incompetent as they will not learn from mistakes.

4 Too much involvement in the job. This happens where managers are more confident in doing the *subordinate's* job. (i.e. they cannot relinquish their *old* job.)

5 Afraid of making information available. Some managers prefer to hold on to all information in order to reinforce their feeling of power.

6 Laziness. The manager cannot be bothered to delegate, thinking it easier to do the job him/herself. This never permits people to learn.

Squares are particularly prone to under-delegation. Being masters of detail they are concerned to ensure that all aspects of a task are carried out correctly – indeed, it was probably because they were so good at this that they obtained promotion to a management position – know they are good at it, and are disinclined to leave it to others. Squares are the sorts who will correct the spelling and punctuation of a subordinate's memo and will cheerfully sit at a computer terminal themselves working out the complexities of budget forecasts. This causes two major problems. In the first place, managers are not managing. They fail to see the big issues, become overloaded with minutiae and suffer stress. And secondly, subordinates feel they have too little to do and are failing to develop any new skills or initiatives.

Curiously, squiggles are also prone to under-delegation, but for different reasons. They are so busy chasing the big issues (some would say seeking the glory) that they often fail to consider others and see whether someone else might provide invaluable advice and expertise. When they do delegate they often do so in a haphazard fashion which confuses the subordinate. 'Back of an envelope' delegation is invariably ineffective and is part of the 'crisis management' that we discussed earlier.

The two shapes that are least likely to be prone to under-delegation are circles and triangles; the former because they consider people and are likely to think about the individual needs of subordinates, and the latter because they can adopt a long-term, global view, are good at planning and possess a strong awareness of political developments. This seems another instance where 'opposite shapes' actually have something in common.

Over-delegation
The final situation is where too much responsibility is passed to other people.

Over-delegation can occur because:

1 Managers may lack experience in the job. They may be timid and happy to let others undertake the tasks.

2 They may be poorly motivated to do their own job. They may be lazy, and happy for others to do the work.

3 They may be afraid of making errors themselves and anxious not to appear incompetent.

4 Subordinates may *encourage* the situation as they are keen to take over the manager's job.

   In short, over-delegation is likely to occur where a manager, for one reason or another, feels insecure in his/her job. Moreover, the situation is likely to be intensified where there is a more able subordinate angling for the job. Others in the workteam will feel that the manager cannot do the job and that tasks are unfairly passed on to them when they lack the necessary expertise. All this will create bad feeling, especially if things go wrong and the manager chooses to blame the workers.

   No particular shape seems more or less likely to indulge in over-delegation: it seems to depend on circumstances. Any shapes could, given an insecure situation, find themselves delegating too much.

Conclusion

This chapter has been concerned with the important topics of time management and delegation as they relate to management control. My central theme has again been that there are no clear 'commandments' and that it comes down to a consideration of individuals and their particular management styles. Much time management instruction seems to me to be in the 'how to keep your desk tidy' tradition; is over-simplistic and easily appears to many managers as 'ticky-tocky'. In fact, time management training is invaluable, but it is far less concerned with diaries and checklists than with *self-analysis* – each person understanding his/her own particular strengths and weaknesses. Study the checklists by all means, but don't consider them to be laws set in stone. Rather, consider your own management style, understand your shape, and take from the checklists what appears to be appropriate.

10 Communication and coordination

In our discussion of the management cycle (Chapter 2) we placed 'communication and coordination' at the centre. These were the central core activities that tied the others together. All the different management activities – planning, decision making, organizing, negotiating, leading, motivating and controlling – need to be coordinated, and this is largely achieved through communication. In this chapter I will look at each in turn, beginning with communication.

The nature of communication

People in work organizations constantly complain of 'breakdowns in communication' or 'poor channels of communication' and you often hear particular managers described as 'poor communicators'. I even recall an occasion when I was asked by a senior manager to arrange for someone to go on a course because 'he couldn't communicate' and 'needed communication skills' – as though a one day course would, like a course of antibiotics, suddenly solve the problem! The truth is that any manager can communicate. Psychologists have shown that even babies born blind and deaf rapidly develop means of communication: this is common to all humankind. The point about many managers is not that they 'cannot communicate' but that they communicate so badly.

Communication involves three key aspects: content, code and channel.

★ The content is the *information* that one person wishes to transmit to another. This includes *what* is being communicated, i.e. the content.

★ The code is the *manner* in which the message is conveyed. In other words, it is *how* the message is transmitted – the facial expression, tone of voice, etc.

★ The channel is the *vehicle* selected for transmission. This involves deciding the means of transmission, i.e. *where* the message is to be placed – in a letter, at a meeting, on the phone, through a computer network, etc.

The problem for many managers is that they often use the wrong channel for the content, i.e. some *always* write; some *never* write. The art of management is to identify the most appropriate channel for communication: to know when a formal letter is required, when a quiet word is more appropriate, and so on. A key point to bear in mind is that there is often 'noise' or 'interference' in the communication process. This may be internal (e.g. the receiver is tired, preoccupied, etc.) or external (e.g. machinery, traffic, aircraft, etc.). Effective communication, therefore, involves far more than just the content of the message.

STAGES IN COMMUNICATION

There are six main stages in the communication process. The first of these involves the content; the second and fifth, the code; and the third and fourth, the channel. The final stage synthesizes the whole process.

1 *Conceiving the message to be communicated* The first stage is for individual A to decide *what* is to be communicated to others.

2 *Encoding the message into the form in which it will be transmitted* Individual A has to decide on the manner in which the message is to be transmitted. This will also, inevitably, involve a choice of channel but the point is that the *manner* in which the message is sent will be viewed by the receiver in a particular way. If, for instance, individual B receives a formal letter concerning a matter he or she regards as meriting little more than an informal word, certain things will be read into it.

3 *Selecting the communication channel* Individual A must then select the most effective channel for the communication (i.e. the postal system, the telephone system, etc.). This will include a consideration of further factors besides how it is received by the other person (e.g. speed of transmission, reliability of delivery, etc.).

4 *Receiving and interpreting the message* Communication is a two-way process and it is essential that the receiver effectively obtains the information. If B cannot read A's writing, or cannot hear A on the phone, then the process becomes distorted and the content is inaccurately transmitted. This constantly occurs in management communication.

5 *Interpreting the message* It is not enough for individual B merely to receive and understand the content of the message. B is bound to ask questions, albeit subconsciously. Why have I been sent this information now? Why is it sent in a formal letter? Who else has received it? It is important that individual A has considered the way the message will be perceived by B, for B will try and decode it to extract the intended meaning.

6 *Feedback – to indicate that the message has been received and interpreted* The stage that makes the whole process complete is when B indicates to A that the message has been received, understood and interpreted in a particular way. This will almost certainly lead to further messages – of clarification, amplification, modification, etc. – for, though we have identified six main stages, any communication process is continuous and on-going.

With regard to a work organization, therefore, communication can be considered as 'the means whereby people exchange *information* and transmit *meanings* regarding the operations of the enterprise.' I have emphasized the two key words, and each is as important as the other. Communication is not just about *exchanging* information: the receiver will *interpret* the message and if this occurs in a way that was not intended then effective communication, from the sender's point of view, has not taken place.

Communication in organizations

Many management textbooks cover the development of communication skills and making workplace communication more effective – and the manager unquestionably has a whole host of options, both formal and informal, at his/her disposal – but the truth is that there are limits to how effective organizational communication can be. Despite the constant pleas one hears for 'open participation', 'democratic management', 'widespread consultation' and the like, in reality, work organizations are highly political places and, despite the rhetoric, no one is ever completely open. The truth is that organizational life encourages us to give incorrect feedback, to be less than honest, to pander to our superiors while neglecting subordinates; in short, to play a multitude of political games. And the irony is that we would not wish it otherwise. As we are all less than perfect, we actually *need* laundered messages, filtered feedback, even deliberate lies, to protect ourselves and avoid hurting others. This dilemma points to the central conflict within any organization – the clash between 'me' and 'the system'. The system may be designed to encourage unfiltered, open communication but, counterbalancing that, each of us wants privacy and protection.

All this explains why managers so often complain about 'problems' of communication. It is not just that there are problems with departmental jargon, individual handwriting and the noisy open plan office – though these may be bad enough – but, equally important, people are constantly attuned to the political undercurrents and will obtain and launder information in devious ways. Information from certain departments and managers will always be received with certain preconceptions (i.e. stereotyping) while one or two pieces of information may be used to generalize about a larger situation (i.e. the 'halo effect'). As a result of these and other practices information is continually concealed, held back, doctored, leaked and distorted. Perfect communication is simply not an organizational reality.

Forms of expression

Because of these factors I see little point in courses on 'How to become an effective communicator' or 'How to open up communication in your company'. Such titles are misleading. One can certainly *improve* communication but we are back to our recurring theme that there is no one set of specific skills that can be learned; there is certainly no hope of obtaining perfection; and the key point, once again, is that people are *different* and, therefore, communicate in different ways. The important thing is to try to understand the subtleties of human interaction and the ways in which people vary their approach as they communicate with others.

I want, therefore, to focus discussion at the individual level and investigate how the *application* of the communication stages are adjusted as the process develops. This relates to any form of communication but I shall focus in particular on verbal communication, the main form used by most managers.

If we analyze conversations we discover there are four kinds of expression:

1 *Observations* This involves reporting what your senses tell you. You need to be precise and accurate and acquire the language of the scientist or detective.

2 *Thoughts* Your thoughts are conclusions, inferences, etc. drawn from what you have read, heard and observed. They are attempts to synthesize observations. Beliefs, opinions and theories are all examples of thoughts.

3 *Feelings* Everyone needs to grieve, be angry, get upset, etc. but this is made

difficult if it is not encouraged by the other person. We should always allow others to express their feelings.

4 *Needs* We need to let others know what our needs are and allow them to express their needs to us. As with feelings, this may not be easy, but we should not assume (as many do) that others know our needs or that theirs are the same as ours.

A key point is that observations can be considered as *facts* while the other three involve *opinions*. All conversations are a mixture of facts and opinions; one is used to support the other, and vice versa. We need opinions to back facts and facts to support opinions. For instance, we might say 'our competitors have reduced their costs; therefore we must do the same' (fact followed by opinion) or 'I think we should reduce our costs; our competitors have done so' (opinion followed by fact). In conversation with others, therefore, we should demand facts to support opinions and ask for opinions, given certain facts. It should be noted, however, that in some instances the situation becomes distorted if people use facts to, in reality, express opinions. This is common between husbands and wives. A statement like 'I see you're wearing that old brown jacket again' may be a statement of fact but it is, of course, being used to offer an opinion!

GENERALS AND SPECIFICS

Both facts and opinions can be used in a *general* or *specific* way. For instance, 'I think I need a cup of tea' is a specific opinion while 'I think motor vehicles are dangerous' is a general one. And just as facts and opinions are used to support each other, so are generals and specifics. Salesmen are particularly adept at this. They often begin by asking a general question (e.g. 'How much money do you think people lose each time they shower?') as a way of getting the other person to focus on their own specific situation (i.e. how much money are *you* losing?). The result of the exchange is that you realize you are losing more money than you thought and, presumably, will purchase a new shower head.

This allows us to draw a matrix – between facts and opinions and those that are general and specific (Fig. 10.1). The art of good conversation is to move in and out of the four cells in accordance with the other person. This involves the skills of diverging (opening up) and converging (closing down) which provide control in a conversational setting. With diverging (making things more diverse) we move from facts to opinions and from the specific to the general, while with converging we move in the opposite direction.

We often begin by diverging (e.g. stating broad opinions based on certain facts) but then converge, usually in response to the other person, as various opinions are compared and new facts established. As a result of the convergence it should be possible, finally, to make a decision.

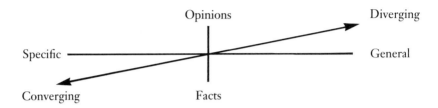

Figure 10.1 Different forms of expression in conversations

If one relates this to a meeting situation, the key rules for managers would appear to be:

1 Having stated the problem, collect the available facts from everyone.

2 When people give opinions, ask for evidence to back them up.

3 When people give facts, ask them what they feel are the implications.

4 When someone gives a fact/opinion that seems rather personal (i.e. specific) ask how others feel about it (i.e. diverge opinion).

5 When people exhibit strong feelings, summarize what they have said and ask for supporting evidence (i.e. diverge facts).

6 When people ramble or pontificate, bring the meeting back to the agenda (i.e. move to specifics).

One could no doubt continue this checklist. The art – and good communicators do it instinctively – is to move in and out of these cells at the appropriate moment. Major problems can arise, however, if one person remains in a 'specific facts' situation – continually producing information relevant to the task in hand but never offering an opinion – while the other only voices 'general opinions', and is constantly preaching about the world and all its problems but never supports these views with any hard evidence. In such a situation both persons end up talking past each other – and probably regarding each other as 'poor communicators'. Self-assessment tests are now available which allow managers to identify whether they are poor at either diverging or converging. This information can be useful for it enables us to identify weaknesses and to improve our skills at either opening up discussions, offering opinions, etc. (diverging) or sticking to the point, keeping to time, etc. (converging).

The reader will have noticed that, once again, the four shapes of our management matrix correspond with Fig. 10.1. Squares are the great convergers – concerned for detail, good at sticking to the point, adept at relating general remarks to the specific situation, but poor at opening up the debate and offering opinions. Triangles, by contrast, are far more general in their remarks – with their ability to take a long-term view – but are still inclined to focus on facts rather than opinions. Opinions are more likely to come from the people-focused circles, particularly where they relate to work colleagues and those immediately affected by any decisions. Broad, even outrageous, opinions are more likely to come from squiggles. These are often unrelated to the issue under discussion, not supported by facts, and often of a highly personal nature. The problem in meetings is often to keep squiggles focused, however entertaining their ideas might be, on the matter in hand.

Coordination

The second key word at the centre of the management cycle, coordination, I shall deal with fairly swiftly for it merely means the bringing together of all the other aspects of management behaviour we have considered so far. It is the linchpin for everything else and provides us with an overview of a manager's performance.

Charles Margerison (1986) suggests that the overall effectiveness of managers can be judged in terms of

(a) their ability to manage and

(b) their level of competence.

The ability to manage relates to handling people while competence refers to an individual's breadth of experience and expertise. Using these two variables, Margerison produces the following matrix and four roles, which I shall consider in turn (Fig. 10.2).

(a) *The Specialist* has a narrow range of experience and may well be expert in a particular field, but Specialists often have a low inclination to manage others and find the thought of administration unappealing. Their key interest is in pursuing what they know best. They often like to do their own work in their own way with the minimum of interference. Specialists are very important in research and development, in planning jobs and in other technical work requiring deep concentration and considerable expertise. Such people, however, are unlikely to make successful managers. They have neither the inclination nor the experience.

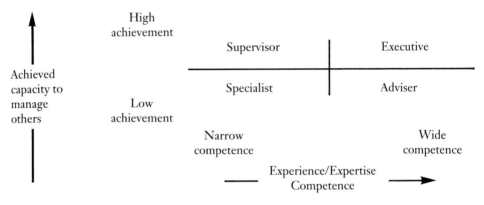

Figure 10.2 Types of role within organizations

(b) *The Adviser* too has a fairly low concern for managing others but (unlike the Specialist) operates across a wide field of experience and knowledge. An Adviser works with a variety of clients and can be viewed essentially as a 'consultant', offering expert advice on a range of topics (e.g. the accountant who has a wide knowledge of various financial systems within a company). The adviser, therefore, has broad experience but little interest in managing subordinates.

(c) *The Supervisor* is interested in people and has a high capacity to manage them, but only within prescribed limits. Supervisors enjoy administering tasks but only do so within specific and limited areas of knowledge and experience (e.g. production supervisors). They are unlikely to venture beyond their traditional area of technical training.

(d) *The Executive*, by contrast, is the person who understands the other three roles and coordinates them into an approach that we might term 'general management'. Executives have a high capacity for gaining achievement through managing others. They have probably held the other roles previously and will have used this experience to broaden their management expertise. Their broad-based competence enables them to assess organizational issues on a broad front.

Margerison is not suggesting that one role is better than another; simply that they are different and that each has a part to play in providing an effective management team. It can be seen that our management matrix also fits Margerison's work and that his four types correspond to our shapes. Specialists are essentially squares and, if they want to become skilled managers, need to broaden their experience and become Advisers. Similarly, Advisers need to gain management experience as Supervisors while Executives require experience of all three roles. This is similar to the suggestion I made in Chapter 8 that our top managers should be more like film directors (high on creativity and autonomy) than team players or company planners.

We have now circled the management cycle, covered the main functions that managers are expected to perform, and concluded the discussion by considering communication and coordination. In the final chapter we ascend from the individual to the organizational level and consider whether a particular shape seems likely to become the dominant form in the future. What, in other words, is the shape of things to come?

11 The shape of things to come?

So far we have used the management matrix as a vehicle to analyze different forms of behaviour on the part of individual managers. We have seen how it can be used to study learning, decision making, group dynamics, negotiation, leadership, motivation, time management, communication and coordination. In this final chapter we bring these various activities together to consider the manager within the context of the work organization.

Might we expect that, just as individual managers operate in different ways, so *organizations* will adopt particular cultures – sets of values, norms and beliefs – and function in differing ways? After decades of management theorizing and training one might have thought this was unlikely. Might we not expect one ideal form of workplace structure, one best way of motivating employees, one best way of reaching decisions, etc.? Sadly, the whole of this book shows this to be impossible. We have seen how different managers are from each other and, given that work organizations are made up of individuals, we can expect them to be different too.

Organizational cultures

In his stimulating book *Gods of Management* (1986) (and his other book, *Understanding Organizations* (1983)) Charles Handy suggests that work organizations develop distinctive cultures and operate in particular ways. These cultures involve deep-seated beliefs about the way work should be organized; the way authority should be exercised; and the way people should be rewarded and controlled. Indeed, the different cultures can be further subdivided into sub-cultures, for different functional departments will develop their own ways of doing things – a fact we have noted at various times throughout this book.

To provide some order to these differences, however, Handy suggests there are four main cultural forms which pervade workplaces, and graphically illustrates these by relating them to four of the gods of ancient Greece. The possible cultures he labels power, role, task and person.

The power culture

This culture is frequently found in small entrepreneurial organizations, traditionally in the robber-baron companies of nineteenth century America, occasionally in today's trade unions, and in some property, trading and finance companies. The patron god of this culture is *Zeus*, the all-powerful head of the gods of ancient Greece, who rules by whim and impulse, by thunderbolt and showers of gold from Mount Olympus.

The power culture depends on a central power source – a visible, charismatic figure who dominates the organization. The organization works on precedent, on anticipating the wishes and decisions of the leader. There are few rules and formal procedures, and little bureaucracy. Control is exercised from the centre largely through the selection of key personnel but also by the occasional visit from, or summons to, the centre.

As a style of management, this closely corresponds to the approach of the squiggle. These cultures allow people to move quickly (even if they often move in the wrong direction!) and appeal to those who seek risk-taking and excitement rather than security and order. Zeus individuals tend to think intuitively, relying on impressionistic 'soft' data (e.g. gossip, hearsay, feelings, etc.) in preference to conventional, hard reports, and to see things as wholes. They are good at viewing the whole picture but can quickly become bored with detail. They learn by trial and error or modelling rather than in a formal sense and are far more interested in what others are doing than in current theory. Such managers synthesize rather than analyze and it is a style common among chief executives.

Handy believes that size can become a problem for such organizations: the web of interpersonal links can break and bureaucracy become a necessity. The best approach seems to be for power cultures to spawn other offshoots (e.g. subsidiary companies) with financial control remaining as the string that binds them.

In short, these cultures put a lot of faith in the individual (succession can prove a problem) and little in committees. Whom you know is far more important than what you know and political sensitivity is an essential requirement. Considerable time is spent creating and maintaining networks and many key decisions are made over lunch or at the golf club. Zeus-like organizations are invariably seen as tough, abrasive and successful, but often exhibit low employee morale and high turnover rates. They are exciting places to work in, but not very comfortable.

The role culture

The role culture is often stereotyped as bureaucracy and the patron god is Apollo, the god of reason, order and roles. This culture works by logic and rationality and its strength lies in structure – clear departmental responsibilities, job descriptions, functional specialisms, etc. The various subsections are coordinated by a narrow band of senior management. It is assumed that this is the only personal coordination needed, for structural arrangements should ensure that the different departments do their job. Indeed, it is interesting that, in this culture, the role (or job description) is generally more important than the individual who fills it. Each job is clearly specified (so that various people can fill it); indeed, performance over and above what is prescribed is not required, and can even prove disruptive. Position power is the major power source in this culture; personal power is frowned upon. In this culture the manager is the person *in* authority, whereas a Zeus manager *has* authority. The emphasis is on *administration* rather than decision making. Rules and procedures are the main forms of influence, not individuals. For instance, to change the organization one must change the structure and systems rather than the personnel. It will be seen that the prevailing style of management closely corresponds to that of the square. Order, duty, discipline, predictability and obligation are the overriding concerns. Apollonians will find Zeus people crude, irrational, erratic, even frightening at times, while a Zeus will chafe under an Apollonian regime and forget to trust their own intuition or network. An Apollo can often be useful to a Zeus superior, but Apollonian systematic procedures must be understood and tolerated.

It is in this culture that people are often referred to as 'human resources' – resources that can be planned, scheduled, deployed and reshuffled like any other physical asset. It is a culture that encourages such formal techniques as manpower planning, assessment centres, appraisal schemes, training needs diagnosis, training courses, etc. – at least as far as the lower echelons are concerned. One often finds that, at the apex, a Zeus-cum-Athena culture is more prevalent: in other words, the bureaucratic procedures that top managers install do not apply to themselves. Role cultures can survive very effectively in stable environments: where the organization can control its environment, where the market is predictable and controllable, or where the product-life is a long one, then rigid bureaucracies can continue over long periods. The weakness of such cultures is that they are slow to perceive a need for change and slow to change even if the need is seen. They can offer security and predictability; they rarely offer variety and excitement.

The task culture

The task culture is job- or project-oriented. It is the culture of the group (within which the overriding values of democracy and meritocracy are encouraged) and the appropriate god is Athena, the goddess of wisdom and strategy. These cultures work best when a heterogeneous group of talents can find homogeneity through identification with a common cause, task or problem. People do not simply fill pretermined roles but leaders recruit teams and individuals apply to join groups. Where it is predominant in an organization you often find a matrix structure with employees focused on the completion of long-term projects rather than any individual leader. (The Parthenon is a fitting memorial to Athena.) Where leaders do exist they will only be respected for their wisdom and expertise. There is a lot of talk, argument and discussion – endless policy documents are circulated and are expected to be read – and rational justification is seen as the main vehicle for getting one's way. The emphasis is on 'getting the job done', solving problems and taking decisions. Here we see a style that is similar to that of the triangle.

A common tactic in such organizations is 'boxing the problem' – identifying a particular problem and allocating staff time and resources to deal with it – whereby a new box is effectively added to the organization chart (i.e. the title of the box is the problem that needs considering). In this way task groups, working parties, specialist committees, etc. come and go as concerns and issues change in a highly fluid environment. The culture seeks to link the right people with appropriate resources, and let them get on with it. The emphasis is on resourceful humans rather than human resources: people are a dynamic force, responsible for their own destinies. Influence is based on *expert* power rather than position or personal power and is more widely dispersed than in other cultures. The culture is team-based and extremely adaptable; people respond quickly to changing circumstances; feel they have a high degree of control over their work; and base their respect for colleagues on ability rather than age or seniority. Success, to Athenians, is desirable if it has been earned. Such people see Zeus people as over-privileged and lucky, and, while they may admire their forcefulness on occasions, feel they too often act without sufficient thought and deliberation. Apollonians are seen as useful but boring, desiring to preserve the present rather than explore the future.

The task culture, therefore, is appropriate where flexibility and sensitivity to the market are important factors. You will find it where the market is competitive, where the product life is short and where speed of reaction is important. Its weakness, however, is that it does not easily provide economies of scale; does not create great depths of expertise; and is far from easy to control. Top management retains control by allocating projects, people and resources, but this will not work well in large-scale organizations keen to monitor activities. In the task culture vital projects are simply given to good people with no restrictions on time, space or materials. Tight, day-to-day control would violate the norms of the culture. These cultures, therefore, tend to flourish when the climate is agreeable; where the product is all-important and the customer always right; where the market is expanding; and where resources are available for all who can justify using them. Top managers are then free to operate a 'light touch': to relax day-to-day control and to concentrate on strategic decisions. If times become difficult, however, task cultures can prove expensive – they are staffed by experts who like to talk together a lot and talking costs money – and have a tendency to become role or power cultures (i.e. they become more bureaucratic or a new 'big white chief' comes in to reorganize the company).

Athenians are concerned with their own self-advancement, but in a professional rather than a hierarchical sense. They are 'cosmopolitans' rather than 'locals' – oriented to their profession rather than the organization that employs them – and they wish to be recognized for their professional expertise. An Athenian is concerned to 'complete the task', by whatever means; unlike the Apollonian, who is anxious to 'do the job' – correctly, on time and within budget. The task culture is the preferred choice of most middle and junior managers and is advocated in many organizational theories for it emphasizes groups, specialist expertise, rewards for results, etc., but it can prove expensive and will not operate effectively in all circumstances.

The person culture

With this culture the individual is the central point and, though it is not found in many organizations, a lot of people still adhere to its central values. These are represented by Dionysus, the god of wine and song. The key point with this culture is that any organization structure only exists to serve the interests of the individuals within it. Barristers' chambers, architects' part-nerships, academic communities, hippy communes, etc. often enjoy this 'person' orientation. Any structure is as minimal as possible – the organiza-tion is more a *cluster*, or a galaxy of stars – and people regard each other as colleagues or partners rather than subordinates and superiors. Control is by mutual consent and the organization has little power to evict anyone. Influence is shared and the power-base, if needed, is usually expert (i.e. individuals do what they are good at and are listened to on appropriate topics). Like Zeus characters, Dionysians want to make a contribution to the world but it does not have to be 'high profile'. A poem, a painting, even a caring gesture can provide true satisfaction. It is, of course, an environment in which we can expect circles to feel very much at home.

Despite the good intentions of those who advocate this culture, however, the fact is that person cultures invariably move (as the organization becomes established or as a response to economic pressures) towards, at best, a task culture and more often a power or role culture. Handy concludes that many individuals who advocate a person culture often work in organizations that pull them away from this (e.g. the professor who has to suffer the university's increasing bureaucracy). Specialists in organizations – computer people in manufacturing companies, consultants in hospitals, architects in local government, etc. – are also cosmopolitans, like their Athenian counterparts, and will resent their professional freedom being constrained by organizational requirements.

The management matrix

In a part of his book that is of particular interest for our purposes, Handy refers to Eysenck's personality matrix (as we did in Chapter 1) and questions whether his four gods can be fitted on to Eysenck's model. I'm not sure that they can – I'm not sure a Dionysian should be described as unstable and introverted – but it is interesting that Handy is searching around for a framework that allows him to relate the gods to each other. Eysenck's model is too broad for our purposes – if managers were 'neurotic introverts' they simply wouldn't be in the job – but our management matrix does appear useful. If we replace extravert-introvert with high and low assertiveness, and stability with emotion, then we find that Handy's four gods do correspond to the different cells (Fig. 11.1).

The Apollonian role culture I have labelled 'Bureaucratic' for obvious reasons: it is strongly task-oriented and inward looking in that its primary concern is with the efficient working of the internal organization. This is very much home territory for squares. The person culture I have termed 'Collegiate' for it corresponds more to the senior common room of the academic world: while it is still inward looking, it is far more strongly people-focused. The task culture, as we saw, is based around long-term projects with people grouped in expert teams. The culture is very much task-focused but the organization is more able to adapt swiftly to changing external circumstances. It is, therefore, more outward looking and the culture of the triangles. The power culture – which is both people-focused and outward looking – I have labelled 'Entrepreneurial', for such organizations are invariably centred around a visible leader, accompanied by an entourage of loyal disciples. It is an atmosphere in which squiggles thrive.

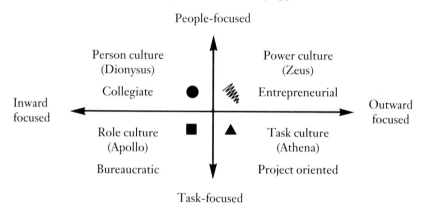

Figure 11.1 Different forms of organizational culture

Most workplaces will, of course, be a mix of these, with sub-cultures emerging within the overall dominant culture. The factory where I work, for example, employs some 5000 people and, while I would not claim that it fits neatly into any of the four categories, parts of it certainly do. The Technical function (where the aeroplanes are designed) has a strong task culture. Highly trained, expert staff work in teams on long-term design projects and circulate between various project teams both at our site and between other parts of the company. Many have bosses who are located in other parts of the country (so the amount of direct personal supervision is not great) and most will feel more oriented towards their particular area of expertise, the aerospace industry or a specific product, rather than the site where they happen to work. The Production Department, on the other hand, (where the planes are manufactured) is far more a role culture. Hierarchy is strong and people fill predetermined slots in a highly bureaucratic fashion. Areas such as Business Systems, Project Management and Human Resources, in contrast, purvey more of a collegiate feel while some senior management groups come closer to power cultures.

Influencing factors
Handy proposes four 'principal forces' that determine which cultural form
(or mixture of forms) an organization is likely to take:

(a) *Size* Only the role culture does not depend on people knowing each
other; therefore this (more bureaucratic) form is more likely to be found in
very large organizations. Ten seems to be the breakpoint. Once you have
more than ten individuals in a group, ten groups in a division, or ten divisions
in a company, then you have to rely on more formal methods of control and
coordination.

(b) *Life-cycles* The greater the rate of change, the more likely it is that a
task culture will emerge. Athenians will come to the fore and set up working
parties, call in consultants, prepare special reports, etc.

(c) *Work patterns* There are three main ways in which work can be
organized:

1 The *flow* pattern – where one section's work leads into another (e.g. a
production line, chemical process plant, local authority, etc.).

2 The *copy* pattern – where the work of each section is identical (e.g. branch
banking, travel agents, etc.).

3 The *unit* pattern – where the work of each section is independent (e.g. a
self-employed potter, family farm, etc.).

Flow and copy patterns encourage role cultures while unit patterns are more
Zeus-like, Athenian, or even Dionysian. This explains why the takeover of a
small firm (with a power or person culture) by a big firm (with a role culture)
can prove such a painful experience: people undergo culture shock as they are
forced to adjust to a new environment.

(d) *People* Different people are inclined towards different gods, and
organization cultures will be affected by the make-up of the people within
them. Moreover, once a distinctive corporate culture emerges the organization is likely to recruit people of a certain type – thus perpetuating its style.
Some of the people influences are well known: young people are less likely to
be Apollonian; well-educated people may well be Athenian; innovative
entrepreneurs are more Zeus-like, etc. Any culture is constantly evolving and
the people within an organization help to form it.

The individual and the organization

Handy maintains that his theory helps explain why people may be comfortable or uncomfortable in particular organizations.

'A follower of Zeus will not be happy, or effective, in an Apollonian organization. An Apollonian manager will find Dionysians irritating beyond belief.'

This closely parallels what I have been saying throughout this book. Because managers become entrenched in a certain style, and because organizations come to be dominated by prevalent cultures, people in workplaces become resistant to change even though new circumstances may require new approaches, structures, procedures, etc. This explains 'cultural confusion', which shows up in inefficiency, but more especially slack – the extra resources, long delivery times, increased overtime, overstaffed head office, etc. – which is used by management as a way of cushioning a wrong culture. The message is that managers need to become aware of their own cultural inclinations and more open to the alternative choices that face both themselves and the organization. In his book, Handy provides some self-assessment exercises which allow readers to identify the cultural make-up of (a) their organization and (b) themselves.

CULTURAL CHANGE

Handy believes that a major cultural crisis is affecting work organizations today. He suggests that whether we like it or not – and he concedes that many don't – we are being pushed (by economic circumstances) away from Apollonian bureaucracies to structures that are more flexible and open. This argument is very much in line with other management writers, such as Alvin Toffler (1973) who suggests we are moving from bureaucracy to ad-hocracy, or Tom Peters (1988) who argues that we have to 'thrive on chaos' and learn to love organizational change as much as we hated it in the past. Handy believes we need an 'organization revolution', in which the balance of the gods is changed, that may well prove as significant as the one that accompanied the industrial revolution. The employment organization, centred around the factory or office will give way, he suggests, to a more contractual, dispersed and federal organization in which people work more on a freelance basis. (Information technology makes this increasingly possible.) This will result in smaller businesses, more self-employment and part-time work, and more people working from home. All this will mean a resurgence of Zeus and Dionysus and the decline of Apollo.

Handy believes there is some historical significance in the order in which he places the gods. (After all, Apollo, Athena and Dionysus are all children of Zeus.) Most organizations originated as power cultures – squirearchies built around the personality of the founder, the owner or the patriarch – but role cultures became more prominent with the coming of factory systems. As technology became increasingly sophisticated, specialist Athenian groups emerged, working on long-term projects, and this in turn led to the development of a more collegiate, person culture and the emergence of Dionysus. He concludes that

'If you examine the history of most organizations, you will find they have progressed through the club (Zeus) culture to the role (Apollo) culture, to which they have subsequently added the task (Athenian) and existential (Dionysian) cultures as they have needed to change and develop. By now, most organizations of any size are some mix of all four.'

Much, therefore, depends on 'getting the gods in balance', according to prevailing circumstances. Handy believes, and I agree with him, that organizations face a growing tussle between, essentially, Apollonian and Dionysian values. On the one hand, industrial capitalism has pushed organizations towards greater size and increasing efficiency – which demands the adoption of bureaucratic, Apollonian role cultures – while better educated and more affluent individuals wish to express their ideas and use their skills in a more open, democratic environment (i.e. they would prefer a task or person culture). Handy insists that it is a conflict that will not disappear, and one that Apollo cannot win.

'If our organizations are to survive, they must adapt their managerial philosophy to one which is better suited to the needs, aspirations and attitudes of *individuals*. In the new mix of the gods which will result, Apollo will be less dominant and less inhuman'.

We can conceive the change that is needed as a switch from the employment organization to something more like a professional partnership, a contractual arrangement or a federal state. Treating people as individuals (rather than human resources) requires a culture more akin to the professional association, which is run by consent and individual responsibility rather than decree. Handy believes this is happening. Large organizations are reorganizing to create more federal structures; during the 1980s we witnessed a considerable growth in small businesses; and much management teaching advocates the view that 'small is beautiful'.

Conclusion: the changing matrix

In this book I have used the 'management matrix' to explore the various stages of the management cycle and have now shown, in this chapter, how the four 'shapes' can be related to a discussion of different forms of organizational culture and patterns of change. The various conclusions from each chapter can be summarized in an 'onion diagram' (Fig. 11.2).

I have shown how the work of many influential writers on management – Kolb, Thompson, Belbin, Hersey and Blanchard, Hunt, Margerison, Handy, etc. – can be fitted into this framework. Mine is an approach that argues for *variety* in people and, therefore, management style. It specifically rejects management training which maintains that there are set ways of learning, reaching decisions, leading a team, etc. Management is complex, because so are people. Any attempt to simplify management training is misleading, frustrating and simply dishonest.

I have also insisted throughout that one shape is no better than another – merely different. However, I also maintained that one shape may be more appropriate in particular circumstances and this final chapter – where we have moved up to the corporate level and considered the work organization as a whole – suggests that a new 'mix' is emerging. Without doubt the current message is that bureaucracies must give way to more open, fluid, flexible structures or, to use our terms, squares must give ground to the other shapes. Whether this occurs remains to be seen.

A final word. The reader may feel somewhat bemused by all this talk of 'shapes' and wonder if there's that much in it. Some have commented to me that they are a square on Kolb's test, a triangle on Belbin's and a circle on Handy's. This doesn't particularly surprise me. We must remember that each test is looking at a different *aspect* of management and one may appear square in one context, – say, time management – but more of a triangle with regard to leading others. I would be surprised, however, if managers did not find a fair degree of consistency between their different styles. Managers are unlikely to be a squiggle one moment and a square the next.

Others comment that they are different shapes on the *same* test taken at different intervals; but again, this is to be expected. A constant theme in my book has been that human behaviour is *flexible* and continually changing. Hunt's discussion of motivation illustrates this: i.e. as we grow older we are more likely to pursue the goals of comfort, structure and relationships at the expense of recognition, power and autonomy. The point is that individuals' precise scores are not that crucial. We are painting with a broad brush and

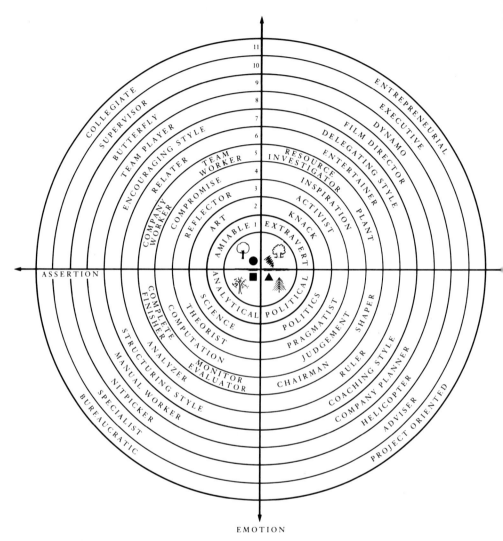

Figure 11.2 The management matrix – a summary diagram

attempting to provide people with an overview of their management style at a particular moment in time. The aim is not to classify them for life!

When people point out inconsistencies in tests they are implying that this renders them inaccurate and meaningless, but this is to miss the point. The value of such tests – and I have suggested in this book that the shapes and matrix offer a useful teaching framework for considering them – is that they encourage self-awareness and help people appreciate the fact that others may not perceive them the way they perceive themselves. This also fits with my view of Psychology. At the end of the day, Psychology (and education for that matter) are not about classifying and labelling people but about helping them to better categorize *themselves*. Would that industry would move away from its obsession with measurement and focus more on development. The aim should be to help people get to like the people they are; to appreciate that others are different from them (but still worth while); and, thereby, to improve their relationships with others.

Bibliography and further reading

Argyris, C. (1975) *Personality and Organization: The Conflict between Systems and the Individual*, New York, Harper and Row.

Armstrong, M. (1990) *How To Be an Even Better Manager*, London, Kogan Page.

Astley, W. G., Axelsson, R., Butler, R. J., Hickson, D. J., and Wilson, D. C., (1982) 'Complexity and cleavage: dual explanations of strategic decision-making', *Journal of Management Studies*, Basil Blackwell, Vol. 19, No. 4, October.

Baldamus, W. (1961) 'Tedium and traction in industrial work', in Weir, D. (ed.) *Men and Work in Modern Britain*, London, Fontana.

Baumgartel, H. (1956) 'Leadership, motivation and attitudes in research laboratories', *Journal of Social Issues*, Vol. 12.

Belbin, R. M. (1981) *Management Teams: Why They Succeed or Fail*, London, Heinemann.

Blake, R. R. and Mouton, J. S. (1962) 'The managerial grid', *Advanced Management Office Executive*, Vol. 1, No. 9.

Buchanan, D. and Huczynski, A. A. (1985) *Organizational Behaviour*, Englewood Cliffs NJ, Prentice Hall.

Cyert, R. M. and March, J. G. (1963) *A Behavioral Theory of the Firm*, Englewood Cliffs NJ, Prentice Hall.

Dellinger, S. E. (1989) *Psycho-Geometrics: How to Influence People*, Englewood Cliffs NJ, Prentice Hall.

Eysenck, H. J. and Wilson, G. (1976) *Know Your Own Personality*, Harmondsworth, Penguin.

Ferner, J. D. (1980) *Successful Time Management*, New York, Wiley.

Fiedler, F. E. (1967) *A Theory of Leadership Effectiveness*, New York, McGraw Hill.

Golzen, G. and Garner, A., (1990) *Smart Moves: Successful Strategies for Career Management*, Oxford, Blackwell.

Handy, C. (1983) *Understanding Organizations*, Harmondsworth, Penguin.

Handy, C. (1986) *Gods of Management: The Changing Work of Organizations*, London, Souvenir Press.

Hersey, P. and Blanchard, K. (1988) *Management of Organizational Behavior: Utilizing Human Resources*, Englewood Cliffs NJ, Prentice Hall.

Herzberg, F. W. (1966) *Work and the Nature of Man*, Cleveland OH, World Publishing Company.

Herzberg, F. W., Mausner, B., Snyderman, B. (1959) *The Motivation to Work*, New York, Wiley.

Honey, P. and Mumford, A. (1982) *Manual of Learning Styles*, London, Honey.

Hunt, J. (1986) *Managing People at Work*, New York, McGraw Hill.

Kolb, D. (1984) *Experiential Learning*, Englewood Cliffs NJ, Prentice Hall.

Lewin, K. (1951) *Field Theory and Social Science*, New York, Harper and Row.

Likert, R. (1961) *New Patterns of Management*, New York, McGraw Hill.

Likert, R. (1967) *The Human Organization*, New York, McGraw Hill.

Lindblom, C. E. (1959) 'The science of muddling through', *Public Administration Review*, Vol. 19.

Little, A. and Warr, P. (1976) 'Who's afraid of job enrichment?', in Weir, M. (ed.) *Job Satisfaction*, London, Fontana.

McGregor, D. (1960) *The Human Side of Enterprise*, New York, McGraw Hill.

McGregor, D. (1966) *Leadership and Motivation*, Cambridge MA, MIT Press.

March, J. G. and Simon, H. A. (1958) *Organizations*, New York, Wiley.

Margerison, C. (1986) 'Planning for management development: managing career choices', in Mumford, A. (ed.) *Handbook of Management Development*, Aldershot, Gower.

Maslow, A. H. (1954) *Motivation and Personality*, New York, Harper and Row.

Mintzberg, H. (1973) *The Nature of Managerial Work*, New York, Harper and Row.

Mintzberg, H. (1979) *The Structuring of Organizations*, Englewood Cliffs NJ, Prentice Hall.

Mumford, A. (ed.) (1986) *Handbook of Management Development*, Aldershot, Gower.

Myers, I. B. and P. B. (1989) *Gifts Differing*, Palo Alto CA, Consulting Psychologists' Press Inc.

Peters, T. (1988) *Thriving on Chaos*, London, Macmillan.

Porter, L. W. and Lawler, E. E. (1968) *Managerial Attitudes and Performance*, Homewood IL, Irwin.

Simon, H. A. (1947) *Administrative Behavior*, New York, Free Press.

Stewart, R. (1967) *Managers and Their Jobs*, London, Macmillan.

Taylor, F. W. (1980) *The Principles of Scientific Management*, London, W. W. Norton.

Thompson, J. D. (1967) *Organizations in Action*, New York, McGraw Hill.

Thompson, J. D. and Tuden, A. (1964) 'Strategies, Structures and Processes of Organizational Decision', in Leavitt, H. J. and Pondy, R. (eds) *Readings in Managerial Psychology*, Chicago IL, University of Chicago Press.

Toffler, A. (1973) *Future Shock*, London, Pan Books.

Tolman, E. C. (1932) *Purposive Behavior in Animals and Men*, Berkeley CA, University of California Press.

Watson, T. (1987) *Sociology, Work and Industry*, London, Routledge and Kegan Paul.

Weekes, D. (1980) 'Organizations and decision making', in Salaman, G. and Thompson, K. (eds) *Control and Ideology in Organizations*, Milton Keynes, Open University.

Vroom, V. H. (1964) *Work and Motivation*, New York, Wiley.

Vroom, V. H. and Yetton, P. W. (1973) *Leadership and Decision Making*, Pittsburgh PA, University of Pittsburgh Press.

Index